The Midworld

by John William Miller

The Paradox of Cause
The Definition of the Thing
The Philosophy of History
The Midworld

in preparation
On the Psychological
Essays: Second Series

The Midworld
of Symbols and
Functioning Objects

John William Miller

W · W · Norton & Company

NEW YORK   LONDON

Library of Congress Cataloging in Publication Data
Miller, John William.
   The midworld of symbols and functioning objects.
   1. Knowledge, Theory of. 2. Universals
(Philosophy) I. Title.
BD161.M458   1982   121'.4   81-19012
                             AACR2

W. W. Norton & Company, Inc.
500 Fifth Avenue, New York, N.Y. 10110
W. W. Norton & Company Ltd.
37 Great Russell Street, London WC1B3NU

1 2 3 4 5 6 7 8 9 0
ISBN 0-393-01579-3

Contents

1   *A Midworld*   7

2   *The Mystery of Appearance*   20

3   *Spectacle and Spectator*   36

4   *Action and Order*   48

5   *Philosophy Is Just Talk*   59

6   *"Explaining" Language*   66

7   *The Act as Unenvironed*   76

8   *The Environment as Actual*   83

9   *The "Presupposition" of Universals*   91

10   *The Form of the Actual*   103

11   *The Actuality of Ignorance*   111

12   *The Constitutionally Incomplete*   118

13   *Facts and Artifacts*   127

14   *Matter*   144

15   *A Few Outlines*   154

16   *A Few Paragraphs*   171

17   *A Catechism for Epistemology*   178

18   *In Sum*   185

1

A Midworld

To begin at the end, as Aristotle recommends, I may say that by the midworld I will be meaning utterance in all its many modes, the locus and embodiment of control and of all constitutional distinctions and conflicts. That, of course, is an end, not a beginning, and the way to that end has not been plotted on a prior and reliable map. I will generalize and say that one has to make one's own way. Goethe said it: "Make your own road."

Philosophy is the discourse without an *"a priori."* All nonphilosophical modes of discourse employ presuppositions peculiar to each. Philosophy has no presuppositions. The end and the beginning are reciprocal. In any story of genesis, the tale is told in terms that have themselves evolved in the process described. The words one uses appear in a dictionary, which is a basic book of genesis, a history book, and not to be scrutinized except on its own terms. There is no prior control for the right use of *all* the words. They have made their way in the speaking.

Stories of genesis are their own warrant. They have no prop, no crutch. Any supposed prop is itself a derivative and resultant of the process that it pretends to warrant. This process I call the *actual,* not an uncommon word and not usually regarded as technical—and all the better for that, although it entails consequences strongly resisted. But let me then say that genesis and actuality are inseparable.

Now, having made a statement about the end, it is necessary to speak of the way to it. This confronts one with the consideration that a genetically produced end must not scorn the base degrees by which it has risen. End and beginning share a common authority, and the end has none with which the beginning was not also endowed. And one faces the consequences that no beginning, discerned by its own evolved end, was or could have been "clear and distinct."

I suggest that all philosophy is biography, a Pilgrim's Progress. In physical science there are no beginnings and no resultants. For biography and history one needs a genetic order. One needs a present. My present requires a totality, a view of the way a here-and-now occurs. To specify Williamstown one needs a map, an extension, a way of asserting a present. Words like the definite article, the demonstrative adjective, the personal pronoun ("the," "this," "I") convey extension. They are what I called "organization words," not "denotative words."

Well, the problem of connectives has been much pursued, as if they were mysterious. It was the problem of "universals."* The mystery lay in the assumption that universals (organization words) were to be "cognitive," like common nouns. Of course they lacked cognitive status analogous to common nouns. So they were accounted for in various ways, as innate, as reminiscence, as *a priori*. On a cognitive basis, they were also sometimes rejected as "pseudo-concepts." They lacked cognitive evidence or derivation.

But if not cognitive they seemed irresponsible. How could one "prove" that $7 + 5 = 12$ or that every event has a cause? On one side, they led to privacy or subjectivism; on the other side, to some totality. So we said "I happen to think in terms of numbers, space, cause, and so forth"; on the other side, we said "The world is spatial, causal, logi-

---

*The universal is not the "identity in difference" about which logicians have spoken. It is not a class name, like "apples," which are not "pears." The universal is in the discriminating procedure, not in what is thereupon distinguished.

cal." In both cases, responsible and verifiable cognition was lacking.

So—speaking very generally—I proposed to accept the arguments against allowing universals cognitive status or force.

If so, one then appears to have abandoned both presence and totality. The very words "here" and "now," as well as the word "and," are organizational. They are universals. Any "this" is *a* "this," neutral to specific qualities. Presence and totality are not cognitive.

What are they then? I called them actual or, if one likes, they are *vox* and *praeterea nihil.* I grasped the nettle. They were *vox* or they were nothing. It is the *vox* that is both presence and the launching pad of totality. They were utterances.

Of course, on a cognitive basis, there is no *vox,* no utterance, no act. So one hears. But on that same basis neither is there the negative "no" or "not." The negative is as much a universal as any affirmation. Universals have been assailed when affirmative; they have not usually included the negative, which is no less lacking in all specific qualities and never appears as an object or as a content of consciousness. The negative is another organization word and, as such, shares the suspicion, or rejection, of all the rest.

I could find, then, no *reason* for any organization word whatever. They all had an immediacy, which gave both presence and totality. But if one says that one "knows" something, one has to offer evidence. Knowledge without evidence is the same as no knowledge. To know is possibly to be mistaken. But the avoidance of mistake is the preservation of a present. If a mistake is another "thing" or object or item of consciousness, why avoid it? If one avoided maple trees for no reason, one would be considered mad, the victim of an irrational fixation, not in charge of one's present. The bottom consideration is rather *what one would be avoiding* if it is a "mistake," another organization item, and so not cognitive at all. Cognition requires at least the possibility of a mistake, yet on its own terms can produce none. A mistake, it has seemed, confused a present and likewise confused a totality.

As a matter of observation, one may note that most people resist both a complete cognitive truth and a complete cognitive mistakenness. This incompleteness is their presence. But they are likewise incomplete apropos of the totality, which permits and enforces an incomplete presence. Totality and presence stand or fall together. Do they? What cognitive evidence supports that statement? None, on the assumption that the universal lacks cognitive probity. Yet, people have been rather insistent about not having cake and eating it too, or in claiming a world constituted in values if there is to be a present wrong, crime, sin, treason, lie. Bearing false witness was regarded as a deep offense, an affront to some totality as well as a dissolution of a present. The question raised by liars is about the man; who is he? It was a strong point with the Greeks.

Of course the assault on cognition has not been restricted to the universal component. In fact, the *content* of consciousness has seemed the very opposite of knowledge, and the "secondary qualities" have been exploited as quite subjective. The "real" tree was not green; it only seemed so. That is a famous story, often told, often retold. On its terms there was neither presence nor totality. The tree of knowledge was not a green tree.

It is rather odd, when one stops to consider it, that common sense persists in crediting a tree with color in spite of the alleged subjective status of quality. This habit of common sense is then attributed to ignorance. The learned know better. What I have not encountered is any explanation of such widespread error. The problem is not, of course, why one would ascribe green rather than red or achromatic quality to the tree; it is rather why one would have been trapped into ascribing *any* quality to it. That the real tree, the cognitive tree, is green because one has been looking (that is to say acting) was not proposed nor that various qualities are discriminated only as one has done something. Looking is a verb. It is not a common noun. It differs from hearing or touching and is classified as "visual" only because one is in control of a functioning and embodied identity. Do nothing and the visual qualities as well as all others lack a common association. All are discrete. Their common feature is a consequence of functioning and of control. It is not a "datum."

At any rate, I accepted the noncognitive status of both presence and totality. That, I think, has become quite respectable in intellectual circles. On cognitive terms there is neither presence nor totality. Presence is now regarded as a superstition, totality as myth. But what, then, becomes of cognition itself? Knower and world disappear. Ignorance, error, and general incoherence become impossible to discover. Where negation vanishes, no cognition, as against ignorance and mistake, can be alleged. The polemic against presence and totality has lost its own leverage. If I cannot be wrong, nobody else can be right, and this presence is not allowed nor is the totality with which I am out of tune. There is, then, no tune and no discord. Cognition commits suicide in rejecting presence and totality on the ground, the sure ground, that they are not cognitive.

I went along with the denial of their cognitive status. I was *not* willing to overlook the denial. I was to be rescued from superstition and myth. Cognition was to save me from errors that no cognitive condition could discover. Instead of clarification, that was annihilation.

So, while I was ready to agree with the nihilists (that presence and totality were not cognitive), I was not ready to abandon cognition itself, especially in view of charges that I had been superstitious and a myth maker, and that I could be rescued from such a deplorable and benighted condition only if I would study physics, psychology, and Bertrand Russell.

Cognition needed a basis, which it could not supply from its own resources. That basis occurs in the repudiation itself; in an action. *The noncognitive basis of cognition is the act.*

The act, consequently, had to meet two conditions: it had to be noncognitive in status, never come upon by the seekers of knowledge, and it had also to be the source and control of all cognition. I had to say that no act will be found among things known, agreeing in this with the view resulting from natural science, from which all verbs have been exorcised. And I had to agree with the psychology of the "stream of consciousness," where there was neither act nor knowledge. I had to go further and say that *as a matter of course* no act would be found in physics, that the absence of act was rather to be expected and could be understood. After all, it is a bit odd to say that one does not "find" or come upon what one could not possibly come upon on cognitive premises. It is not the case that physics "finds" no act, as if it might come upon one but has never done so. Not to find what no looking could disclose is not empirical sense, but nonsense. One could not say what it is that is not come upon. So I was not placidly and passively *agreeing* with the cognitive repudiation of presence and totality. I was *insisting*.

Still, even the act requires some manifestation. No such manifestation can, however, be found among the objects of cognition. That is agreed. What, then, manifests the act and also meets the condition that it be a controller and spur to all knowledge? One needs an object, but not a cognitive object, if one is to find the act.

What, then, are those objects that are not objects of cognition but control cognition? They are *functioning objects.* They are utterances, embodiments, which determine what is known. They are actualities, not realities or appearances. In order to make this point apropos of the most prestigious area of knowledge, namely physics, I early noted and spoke of the yardstick and clock as examples of the functioning object. I could find no characterization of such objects within the limits of physics or chemistry. There is no chemistry of yardsticks, which can be maple, pine, steel, or almost any other substance in the periodic table. They lack all empirical properties of proper objects. Do nothing, and there is no yardstick, clock, balance, number, or word. Do nothing, and the alleged body that is mine, with eyes, ears, hands—with seeing (which is *not* hearing)—do nothing, and it is undiscoverable. But then so is anything else.

Do nothing, and there is no yardstick and the room is not fifteen feet long.

To such functioning objects I gave a name. It was the "midworld." The midworld meets the two conditions: it is not cognitive, and it launches, spurs, and controls all cognition. It is actual. It is not "real." It is not "apparent." *Unenvironed, it projects the environment.*

It got to be trying to hear action relegated to a spook by men who counted, calculated, weighed, and measured in a laboratory, basing a vast story about objects on embodied actualities that were *not* objects of cognition. They said that theirs was the real world, and I thoroughly agreed. But I agreed because it was a world resulting from what was *not* real at all but actual. I was in a bad way because I proposed to save the authority of cognition. And I was proposing to do so by accrediting a yardstick and not a spook.

But beware yardsticks or any other functioning object. For the consequence is a totality, and people say the world is "spatial" on no other warrant than an actuality, which defines a presence and not a cognitive object. Presence and totality stand or fall together. The anti-metaphysics of our day masquerades as an assault on any totality; what it is *equally* attacking is presence, the other side of totality. The center of this obscurantism is the repudiation of the act.

The control of action is the functioning object, not a cognitive object. Similarly the *failure* of control occurs only apropos of such objects, as in fallacy, miscalculation, and bad grammar. A person appears in the act. He does not appear in the "reactions" of behavioral science, which—in order to enjoy the prestige of science—must necessarily avoid dealing in the modes of both presence and totality, that is to say of action. Yet science so invoked as the warrant of reliable discourse is itself the projection of a totality as defined by its own functioning objects. Take away yardsticks, clocks, balances, numbers, controlling words such as "greater than," "atom"; and then logical process and science collapse into the muddle of the unorganized stream of consciousness. It is not the "observer" who directs statements about nature, it is the actual object. *That is why nature is revealed by physics and not by psychology.* Behavioral science is a parasite upon an actuality, which it invokes in order to lay claim to scientific status, but which has no psychological genesis.

We try desperately to become "expressive" and so to appear as present without also declaring the totality that is the formal projection of the moment. We want the *moment,* but not the *momentum.* We want to be heard and seen but resist arithmetic and logic as confining. Any actual moment is also a momentum. Fantasy is the moment that avoids the momentum of its own content. It is the loss of the actual. It is the cultus of feeling that has no consequences. The drug-culture is only incidentally chemical. It is not plausible to suppose that its chemical mode would have assumed present proportions were the temper of evasion not already widespread. Even the arts, whose business it is to raise the moment to an ordered totality, have become "abstract" and therefore inconsequential. What is evaded is not some obscure "reality" but the actual and present. We want motherhood but no actual mother, love without a moral universe. We seek expression but avoid the cultivation of its media. One hears that the "youth" (who, of course, are not young) seek an identity. They wish to be original and "creative," to be effective while treating the actual world with disdain. But they have learned to do so from teachers who say that language is an instrument and mathematics a tool. One is not identified by one's tools. I may never again use my rip-saw. What, then, is the "relevance" of calculus?

The act *declares* the environment and articulates it. The act is *unenvironed.* Functioning does not appear where something called "environment" has been *assumed.* Treat the eye as an object, and there is no looking and no eye to do it. No clock as another object measures time, and with no clock there is no time to measure. It is the barbarian who treats the functioning object as another content of his consciousness. If words are "tools," why not burn the books? The unenvironed object has fallen into disrepute, and properly so. Yet such absolute objects have been proposed as the correlative of an unenvironed present, of an articulate and actual immediacy. Totalities have been attempts to *save a present*. When such a present is not an actuality, not so recognized and declared, then the totality appears as absolute object, not as the form of the actual present. But just as there is no cognition of such absolute objects, so neither is there knowledge of an absolute present regarded as another object. Knowledge turns equally against God and the soul, even against nature as absolute object. There is today a loss of all absolutes as objects. No absolute is cognitive. One had better face up to that. But if cognition be the *basis* for rejecting absolute objects, one had better try to authorize cognition. If one cannot do so, then *all* becomes absolute, every datum a miracle and datum itself unrecognized because unenvironed, with no setting in either a mysterious mind or an equally mysterious world.

The authorization of cognition requires an articulate immediacy, which is the actual, the verb, the counting, measuring, speaking, and much else that is entailed in any presence. We do not act upon objects except as action has already defined objects. "Reaction" does not authorize the scene in which it is alleged to occur. It is a parasite upon the actual world in so far as such prior actuality has not been authorized.

It appears that a moral world is today in disrepute. The scientific world has prestige if only because we are at a loss without electric lights and telephones. Besides, we are dedicated to the auto. We want a cure for the common cold. We even want a free press, not excluding Pandarus and Paul Pry. None of that is available if nobody learns mathematics, physics, and, maybe, even a little logic and some grammar. Perhaps we will learn the hard way that the price of commodity is an ordered immediacy and that the act instead of being a disorderly intruder into the scientific world is rather its source and support. The "disorderly intruder" view of the act has become an axiom of science and is quite proper on cognitive premises. Those who persist in wanting life and action are regarded as anti-intellectual, superstitious, primitive. And in a way they are. But in what way? In the way that treats both present and totality as objects rather than as actualities. If act and life do not define and generate a world, they cannot be found within the cognitive order. We are not even "alienated" on such premises; we are nullified—and any totality along with our own presence.

It is rather curious, though, that while the scientist turns away from the disorderly intruder, he has not been heard to scoff at the current cult of "alienation," which, on his premises, is nonsense. He may even be sympathetic to the "maladjusted" person and offer advice about a better engagement with the "real" world. In fact many scientists itch to put wrong people on the right track. They become "activists" and leave their ivory towers, although no statement in mathematics or physics implies that the times are out of joint or that Washington crossed the Delaware. The solar system is never out of joint. It makes no mistakes or anything else. Nor, on the premises, can the nervous system, as scientific object. But if science does not itself embody local control, any claim to an actual present is in a bad way, because the assault on both presence and totality has been delivered by science. Somehow, though it slay me, yet will I trust in it. If so, I ask for the basis of that tremendous trust, for that alliance with cognition which annihilates the knower and all local control. "How shouldst thou know the knower of knowledge?" There is no knowledge of such a knower, not if he be actual and manifested in functioning objects, in the moment, which is also a momentum.

While my interest was in the act, it was not primarily in science but in history. The status of history was insecure. It dealt in things done, in *res gestae,* not in things perceived. Epistemology, the theory of knowledge, had nothing to say about our yesterdays. It proposed clock-time, but not dated-time, invariance not genesis, the static not the revisory, the uniform not the unique. But it was plain enough that history rode on utterances. You looked for it in records, books, monuments, institutions, in organization and shattering decline. It seemed an outcast so far as it posed as a sort of knowing. No act fell within the limits of cognition as enshrined in our knowledge of nature.

But *perhaps cognition fell within action* and, like history, was a mode of doing. And this suggestion took on force in so far as science claimed to have a history. The strategic move would, then, examine science to see whether its foundations were cognitive or actual. And I believe that to make history authoritative, to rescue it from those who would appropriate it—from theology, physics, psychology—it would be not only strategic but necessary that *res gestae* be present in what seemed not only barren of action but also deliberately and tenaciously perserved from action.

Now *that* is rather odd, that it takes resolution and polemic to clear the cognitive deck of such vagrant intruders. The strength of this resolve was made clear when nature was stripped of all connectives such as cause and, in the case of our pluralists, even of logical order. Nature ceased to have any general order at all. It was then no longer the *order* of nature that rebuked the act, although that had been the original and powerful reason for excluding the act from being known. But if nature had no constitutional order, the case against admitting an act collapsed. Some, like the pluralists, imagined that if they could only shatter the order of nature, they could then make room for the disorderly intruder. But the disorderly act was a boomerang. An unordered doing was more obscure than an unordered nature. One could not so much as count one's fingers or go from here to the post office. Who was William James when he damned the Absolute?

The critics of a constitutional nature were, of course, quite right on their premise of a passive cognition. No factor of order is known. None appears as an item within experience. Space, time, cause, and all the rest never appear. Nobody had said that they appeared. But if they were to be "known," they had to appear. So, they were unknown. They were "pseudo." There was no longer a disorderly intruder since there was no longer any order to be violated. Agent and nature shared a common incoherence. One can-

not tell a pluralist even to mind his *p*'s and *q*'s or enforce
upon him the relation of sides in a right triangle.

But if order is not cognitive, neither is disorder. It is not
perceived. There is no "evidence" for disorder. One is
laughed at today for charging disorderly conduct. The disorderly intruder is disorderly as a violater neither of nature's
laws nor of his own. He can be charged with neither. He
does not act. He only "reacts," and the alleged reaction can
lay claim to no order either in itself or in any supposed
circumstance. This is the admission made by the behavioral scientist, who then proposes to take charge of reactions. If our reactions were part of nature's order, it would
be as foolish to put oneself in charge of them as to propose
to manage the stars in their courses or the stars that had no
courses.

Unless the exorcism of act appeals to an order violated
by act, it has no basis. But on cognitive premises no such
order is discoverable. The exorcism cannot be uttered.

The act appears when any present shows an order of
objects. The first agent was a mathematician. Both his present and his world appeared in utterance, in objects that
had status only functionally, not cognitively; only actually,
not really. All action occurs apropos of this midworld. It
is a control in terms of what has been uttered, a number,
word, line, a temple to Athena or to Notre Dame. In cognition, order has *no vehicle*. That is why it is not found
there. So, to be simple, I emphasize yardsticks and clocks.
They are verbal, not substantive. You handle a yardstick,
you tell a tale, you tell time. But you do not "react" to a
yardstick unless someone uses it as a weapon, and then it
has lost its status and functioning authority, as a commanding and momentous present. It is impious in a deep
sense to treat any item of the midworld as another inconsequential object—the body, or a laboratory instrument,
the idol of the heathen. In fact we now put such idols in a
museum while the critics talk nonsense about abstractions
like symmetry and shadows. Notre Dame was not a stone
mason; she was a poet.

History rides on the midworld. That is why there is a

history of science as functioning objects evolve into their controlled implications, and yardsticks and clocks become related. But objects of perception have no history. Historians do not study the solar system. They study monuments, reminders, not objects of cognition. History *re-minds* us. By the same token it re-minds any totality. "It cometh everywhere." History is not what we happen to do; it is the story of the fatality of doing itself. If science were not based on act, what sense could there be to a history of science? But short of an actual immediacy, or a present and its projected totality, neither science nor history can put in an appearance. And there is much more if we are to return to civility and authenticate our present.

2

The Mystery of Appearance

.

Objects have not usually been accepted as real. They are appearance. Two consequences have resulted: (1) Objects are psychological in status. The rose is not "really red"; it is seen as red, but not always, and not to all perceivers. (2) Objects are manifestations of something underneath, of substance, which is the true reality—and that true reality is not appearance as the object is.

It is notable that no one has regarded an object as real in its own right.

Terms like "real," "apparent," "illusory," and so forth, are not adjectives of a logical subject. They convey a status, not a quality. That the rose is red rather than yellow is determined by looking; that it is "real" or "apparent" is not a consequence of any prior operation. One does not say "Look to see whether or not the red rose is a real rose." The question is not answered by looking for some quality analogous to red or yellow that might or might not be observed by looking.

We have, in fact, been resolute not to give the status of reality to any observed object.

By the same token, neither can we assign the status of appearance to any object because of some observed quality.

Instead of making a mystery of reality, we may make, and we have made, a mystery of appearance.

There is, in fact, a current psychology that endeavors to avoid appearance. Its name is behavioral science.

Nothing is real in its own right; nothing is apparent in its own right. It has been as baffling to move from appearance to reality as from reality to appearance. No account of reality has ever been able to generate appearance; no account of appearance has been able to generate reality. To stand in appearance bars us from reality; to stand in any reality bars us from appearance.

No account of how the distinction of appearance *vs.* reality can originate and be maintained is available in the history of philosophy.

On what basis would one discount appearance (or appearances) as has so usually been done? On what basis would one be suspicious of any reality because it stood apart from appearance, which was its opposite?

Distinctions that are unaccountable in terms of a common denominator, or in terms of their generation, are distinctions without a difference. They are called nonsense.

Yet, in spite of the disjunction, the unmediated disjunction, of appearance and reality, the words are in use by common sense, by poets and theologians. Dated-time is an "illusion"; clock-time is "real." The distinction reappears on the notable authority of Einstein. The real once more characteristically separates itself from appearance, quite as thoroughly as in the One of Plotinus.

Where do they meet?

Look to neither for such a conjunction.

What is it, then, that is neither appearance nor reality but the source of the distinction?

There is no point in looking around for it, as if it were analogous to the red rose in the garden of my aunt. Anything of that sort merely revives the disjunction.

Furthermore, because the appearance-reality opposition is general and pervasive, the common or mediating factor must have the same universality.

Again, because neither appearance nor reality is "known," included in a prior order, neither will the mediating factor be known or be incidental to a prior order.

Again, the mediating factor, the link, the source of the distinction, should be no less familiar than the appearance-reality opposition.

Such are a few of its qualifications.

Most theories of knowledge are diadic in structure. They are expressed as the relation between the subject and the object. Thought "refers" to the object, or thought must be "transcended"; or the object "transcends thought." Such are the modes of expressing the situation in which the problem of knowledge is said to occur. This situation is diadic, a relation between two terms or entities.

Idealism stresses the lack of distinction between subject and object. It has seemed that it sought a monism, and so a disregard of the very situation in which the question of knowledge occurs.

Subjective idealism is a psychological monism or it is nothing. It is really a stream-of-consciousness doctrine. Monism, whether of matter or of spirit, abolishes the problem of knowledge. The "spirit" may be a psychological stream of consciousness, or it may be a divine mind. In neither case is knowledge a problem. And where knowledge is no problem, it has no meaning. To assert that one has knowledge is to claim that thought has been arrested because of its insufficiency. Experience is sufficient for animals but not for men. Knowledge is discovered as self-consciousness and as disparity between the self as experience and the self as reality. Of course, the disparity first occurs as one between the self as experience and the not-self as reality. Here, the self, being only experience, cannot reach the reality, which is valued because that reality cannot be reduced to experience.

The diadic position draws its plausibility from what is true in it, namely that experience must be separated from the true or the real in order to have generated the idea of knowledge. Knowledge can be defined only on the basis of that separation. This is the strength and power of the realistic position.

But now the diadic view has set for itself an impossible

task, namely, that of achieving knowledge in the setting of a division between thought and the real, the psychological and the nonpsychological. Thought seeks its opposite but cannot even recognize that opposite with its own instruments. Thought finds only itself, but what it wants is just the opposite of itself.

Berkeley denied that thought could make any sense out of this opposite. Thought did not so much fail, as go astray in defining its task. One doesn't fail where the quest has no meaning. One has been deceived in supposing there was a quest. That is Berkeley's point. But, of course, no quest at all means no knowledge at all.

The quest must have a meaning. What it can't mean is the reduction of the object of experience to experience. Berkeley refuted realism on the negative point of showing how meaningless and vain was every essay at such reduction.

The Berkeleyan refutation of realism showed that the real could not be the object of knowledge. He showed this by claiming that knowledge has no object. He did not show that the object of knowledge was the perceived object, for the perceived object and the known object are the same in his view. "To be is to be perceived" means that appearance has no object.

Now, it seems that somehow Berkeley must be taken seriously on this point. Knowledge can have no object. Somehow knowledge must be defined as having no meaningful systematic opposite.

At the same time, some alternate for the object of knowledge must be found. It should be conceived in a fashion to preserve the problem of knowledge without, however, so defining that problem as to guarantee the frustration of the quest. The character of that frustration lies in the sort of separation of thought and object that prevents either from discovering or including the other. Thus, Berkeley could not discover the object, while materialism, or even a rationalism of eternal ideas, cannot discover the subject, or its experience.

It should be remembered that the history of philosophy

always shows movements that reinstate experience when either materialism or some variant of objective rationalism discounts the importance of present pain and present laughter. The subjective element keeps coming back. It may be as skepticism, as pragmatism, or as mystical intuition. But it does keep on reaffirming the experiences of the subject.

We must preserve the problem of knowledge. But we must not preserve the problem while destroying knowledge in the posing of the problem about it.

Yet this, I believe, is what has generally been done. It has been done because knowledge has been presented as not the same as experience. It has been presented as something that experience seeks, as the object of experience, as its outcome, or as its completion. Experience has no outcome. It comes to no end. It cannot reach knowledge. If experience is viewed as Humean, that is, as fragmentary and unconnected, no future datum or experience is any better than any present one. One gets nowhere. But, on the other side, if experience be viewed as orderly and connected, then the endless quest likewise gets one nowhere. Knowledge is not the completion of a quest. One would not reach beyond experience that way. Every question would be answered in the same language that asked it, which would be the language of thought, not of truth and reality. It seems necessary, then, to say again that the problem of knowledge cannot mean the termination of a quest. It cannot mean an answer to any question about the relation of experience to something else, or of thought to something else. Such a demand destroys knowledge.

What underlies these frustrations of the diadic form of the problem of knowledge? And what does this way of putting the issue find amiss? It is that experience is not its own ground. That it is not self-defining, not self-explanatory or self-justifying. Experience or thought looks for truth because it doesn't possess it in itself. That is what underlies these frustrations. The shape of the problem declares that in finding truth, thought must not find itself. And, since it can't find anything else, there follows only frustration.

May there not be a clue here? Thought must find itself if it is to find anything at all, including the truth. But in the diadic theory of knowledge, thought in finding itself finds only the subjective. It finds only appearance. These are exactly what it does not want in wanting the "truth."

Thought must find itself, and it finds appearance. Could it be the case that appearance is not what it seeks because appearance is not thought? It is admitted that appearance is not the real; because it is not the real, does it follow that it is thought? Perhaps appearance is neither thought nor reality. That should be considered.

As a matter of fact, there has always been some distinction made between appearance and thought, as well as between appearance and reality. Common sense does not equate appearance with thought. The thoughtful man looks behind appearances. "Skim milk masquerades as cream." And this "thought" has been, moreover, attacked by the defenders of appearance in both ancient and modern times. Thought does not "appear." It would, then, seem a mistake to say that thought cannot find reality in itself because it cannot find it in appearance. Nobody has ever argued the equivalence of appearance and thought, not even Berkeley.

Thought is not exhausted in appearance. Hence, in rejecting the equivalence of appearance and reality, it is not rejecting the equivalence of thought and reality.

As more than appearance, thought has always been presented as form, law, order. This has led to the categories, to the "presuppositions" of experience, to the conditions of appearance, to the *a priori,* the universal.

It is apropos of the universal that appearances get identified. For what appears is now a manifestation of order. The tree "appears" taller or shorter because one assumes the spatial order. Apart from that assumption, no suggestion of a distinction between appearance and reality could be defined. Appearance is no datum. It is not an innocent idea. It assumes the structure exemplified and conveyed in particular experiences. Otherwise each experience would be absolute and not in the least an appearance. Even among the Milesians, appearance secures identification apropos of substance, unity, cause, or genesis. But such ideas are formal. They are "thought," both as substantive and as verb.

So, thought has reached out for more than appearance. It includes more. Thought, now abroad in nature, is no longer subjective. It includes the subjective. It now becomes possible to explain subjective factors of thought, and one need hardly explain at length the exploitation of that possibility by the determinists. Subjectivity can always be "explained"; but that is not at all the same as explaining thought. For thought now reveals nonsubjective factors, precisely those that arouse the positivists and radical subjectivists.

One might like to rest here. One is no longer confined to subjectivity. One is abroad in nature. Thought owns the order of nature.

Very true, but by the same token it no longer owns the content. This is a paradoxical reversal. The content, the data, seemed all too subjective. They were uncomfortably so. But the order that now surrounds them, giving them a measure of intelligibility, has moved them into the nonsubjective. They now have causes and reasons, get measured in location and time. They become accidents of a region of infinite order, accidents in a region that is not subjective. From being accidents of perception they now become accidents in an infinitely ordered nature. Somehow that order generates and accounts for them. This is the setting for the problem of the accidental.

This problem occurs not because there are data in consciousness; it occurs because the accidents have a setting in a nonaccidental region. The problem of the accidental is not the consequence of chaos; it is the consequence of order. It announces the infinity of that order. Out of that infinity arise data. They are not illusion, not fiction, not imagination, but reality. And they borrow that flavor of reality from the nonsubjective status of the order within which they occur. But that order is also the order of thought. If the accidents convey an impression of reality, it is because thought finds what was once appearance to be more than appearance. But this new factor of data or experience is wholly due to thought's finding reality in itself, namely, in order and form. Accidents have only the reality of the order within which they occur. But that reality is not appearance, is rejected by defenders of appearance. It is thought.

Appearance (that is, subjective data) has become reality. Thought has modified the position and meaning of the content of consciousness. Is the tree thought or reality? As part of "nature" it is now so much caught in reality that its appearance to thought has become accidental. In nature the tree is no accident; it is only in thought that it is an accident. No question about the tree as object is intrinsically puzzling. Nature will account for all of it. But it remains a puzzle that nature—as a whole—should include the tree. Out of infinite nature, this tree. That is the vindication of the nonsubjective status of the tree as part of the nature.

The true seemed not in thought. It was something to be discovered as the referent or object of thought. That demand is impossible of fulfillment. Truth eludes thought. Thought does not possess truth in itself, but must look for it elsewhere. It must look elsewhere because thought equates appearance. It was at this point that the tide began to turn. For appearance suggests no need of an object other than itself. The real as other than appearance became an unintelligible demand. Appearance became the same as knowledge, and no counterfeit or substitute for knowledge.

But appearance as equal to reality is not thought. It raises no problems. It is passivity. In equating perception and being, Berkeley omitted thought altogether. The tree existed (it has *"esse"*) but it was neither appearance nor reality. It was not the appearance of reality. Its *"esse"* was its *"percipi,"* and vice versa.

The problem left by Berkeley was the rediscovery of thought, that is, of subjectivity. Berkeley destroyed subjectivity because he destroyed the distinction between appearance and reality.

Subjectivity became reestablished as an aspect of necessary structure. Subjectivity became defined through ideality, that is, through the order of nature. That order was, however, ideal. Hence subjectivity became not a datum but a corollary of thought or reason. It became an aberration of thought from its own canons, not an aberration of thought from reality. Appearances, once viewed as subjective, now became the very reverse, namely, the evidence of nonsubjective reality as ideally ordered and defined. Appearances became part of nature. They were no longer subjective states cut loose from attachment to the nonpsychological, the objective, the real.

In the original position, thought was given the task of finding a reality in which it did not find itself. That task is impossible. True, the reality sought could not be found in appearance. But appearance is not thought, any more than it is reality.

In the outcome, thought did find enough reality to make possible the treatment of appearance as thoroughly and disturbingly real. Thus, appearances raised the problem of the accidental, not as a problem of appearance, but of reality. Now, accidents prove reality, not appearance. They do this because they have status in a nonsubjective order where alone their property of being accidents can be made clear.

Now, however, we no longer have a diadic relation, but a monism. Thought is no longer opposed to reality. It also defines the subjective, or unreal, as a variation from formal order, as error, and as sin. Everything falls within thought. This is roughly the position called absolute idealism. Thought no longer looks for a reality outside of itself.

Thought must not find the real where it does not also find itself. Still, whatever the real, or whatever itself, it must find them. To find them is to do more than passively experience factors of consciousness. That is not a search. In that context a puzzle has no status other than as an experience that comes and goes. Thought must find reality, but it cannot find it by appropriating what seemed alien, by taking over nature or even illusion. Thought in finding itself cannot also find the real by an appropriation of an object. Nor by the appropriation of the region of objects in lawful array.

Berkeley lost the distinction between thought and real-ity. But so did Kant. Kant tried to maintain the distinction but possessed no ground for making it. It was not merely that the noumenon remained a mystery, but that the phenomenal region was equally without intelligible contrast. Confined to the phenomenal, how could he objectify it? And has there not been a question about his *a priori?* Are those forms more than psychological after all? Are they not just the way we *do* think? Do we find them as data? Such questions have been raised. But in so far as thought possesses experience and reality, it reduces them to a vaster alienation than the distinction between thought and reality. The fate of Berkeley is renewed. Thought has not found itself in a revision of the story of experience. True, there are now forms as well as content, but both are factors of appearance, of *bewusstsein,* of consciousness. And the old problem of going beyond consciousness recurs. One does not escape from consciousness by revising its content, or by discovering that the content also has form.

In retrospect it seems almost too obvious that thought would somehow appropriate all objects and the whole region of objects with all the qualities and distinctions displayed by objects. Is it not plain that all that must fall either to Berkeley or to Kant? One has to explain oneself; so, in telling what one finds in objects, one reduces them all, in every way, to consciousness or to thought. But in the appropriation of objects, thought has not found reality. It has in fact not preserved its own meaning. It must seek; it must look for reality and for itself. Consequently, it must do more than report. And what is the story of an object, or of the order of objects, if not just a report? And what is such a report but an elaboration of materials that never could successfully pretend to be more than experience?

This seems strange—that in appropriating objects, or the whole region of objects, thought should not find truth or reality. For, was it not the aim of thought in its search for truth to find itself everywhere? Surely, where it did not find itself it could not find truth but only bafflement. So, it found itself everywhere and has no rival. It takes all meaning to itself, sees all distinction between itself and the object as its own work, sees concepts like "appearance," "subjectivity," "illusion," "knowledge," and so on, as its own work.

What seems amiss in that story? The old objection that the region of objects, or of nature, has become "subjective" can no longer be made. Nature is a region of law, order, and form. As such, it is opposed by subjectivists, by positivists, and by radical empiricists. As orderly and lawful, it exceeds all possible sensation or perception. It is not a state of mind, a "determination of consciousness." It is not a datum. It is not content. It allows derivation and criticism of subjective states of opinion, peculiarities of perception, and so forth. No, it is not subjective. That is not what is amiss. The charge of subjectivity rests on a contrast with an object that is reflected in, but not defined by, experience. But in absolute idealism the difference between subject and object is seen to be itself the work of thought, a formal difference only. Indeed, the vast region of nature, the region of infinite change according to law, is now remote from caprice and immune to being absorbed into appearance. But it is, for all that, a region of thought.

It seems worthwhile, then, to be as clear as possible on the point that absolute idealism cannot be charged with subjectivism. That charge has meaning only on other and more rudimentary premises.

No, the uneasiness here must have a different basis, if any.

There is such a basis. Thought has appropriated its object. It sees itself pervading the object. But this object, or region, does not show thought to itself. It does not show the activity of thinking. It shows no thinker.

The assumption is that thought will always find its own properties indirectly, namely in whatever materials seem to be its abode. When thought was "appearance," it could not find itself in the nonpsychological, in nature and its laws. When thought saw itself in nature, it became impersonal, indistinguishable from the object. It seems always to work out this way. Plato saw thought in the eternal ideas as well as in appearance and left thought confused. Thought takes its complexion from its medium. By itself it has no properties or outlines whatever, for it is the universal. It can only be as clear as the content and form of experience. Thought finds its portrait in its objects.

But when nature is the object of thought, it becomes impossible to find thought in that object. J. B. Pratt used to say that idealism was materialism, and that is what he meant. Thought and its object were one, but the object was not itself any actual thought nor was there any actual thinker.

Nature may be thought, but it is in the first instance just nature. Space may be thought, but it is more obviously the property of objects having to do with their coexistence. And so it goes. One can show that causation is a rational form; yet, in nature causes pertain only to objects. Thought in nature makes only objects clear.

Nature and thought become very closely joined. They come to have the same order and the same content. Having settled for the ideality of nature, one can forget its ideality and focus on its properties as if they were independent of thought. Mathematical order is a good example. The numbers may be pure thought, but one studies *numbers* and may be surprised to be told that numbers occur only as thought. They *seem* to occur in the context of operational rules, by counting, adding, and so forth. It seems to be precisely thought that is not found in nature. Everything else is there, but not thought.

Now how can thought come to be an object to thought? What is the situation where one supposes oneself to be dealing directly with thought? For, it seems now that to have the object reflect thought is not enough. Thought finds its portrait in the object, but has thought no original? Are there only portraits? A portrait without an original sitter seems odd. And, after all, no one has yet observed the sitter. The portrait is alleged to be there and to be a faithful likeness. But how does one know? The original never appears among the things known or in the region known.

This is not really to be wondered at. If one thinks back over the career of this argument, one finds that the original of the portrait never did put in an appearance. He remained in the background. The appearances, which seemed to fall short of reality and truth, were appearances of objects. Thought was said to refer to objects, or to require transcendence. But it was not to find the thinker that this direction was laid down. It was to find the object of his thought, so that he would have the object, and not just the thought of the object. The quest for the truth began as the quest for the object to which thought referred, or of which appearance was the equivalent in thought. The development of nature occurred because thought was not fully described in appearance. So appearance took on other aspects of thought, became lawful and formal, and so expanded into nature. But an appearance now referred to that natural order. Its truth was found in its linkage with all ordered appearances. The region of ordered appearances became the region of objects. In that region there are only objects. However much one insists that the region of nature is in fact a region of thought, of ideality, one does not thereby remove the realization that every item in the region is an object, that no item is a thought or a subject. But such a result is only what the original problem prescribed. For that problem was that of abolishing the distinction between thought and its object. And that is the result which has been achieved. So far as it goes it was a notable result.

It was noted at the outset that the idea of "knowledge" required a problem. There can be no knowledge, nor any question of knowledge, where the distinction between thought and its object becomes obscure or meaningless. But in the penetration of thought into nature, where is the contrast between thought and its object? It has been lost. It must be recovered.

The clue to the method of the recovery has been given. One must find thought as object. The idealization of nature has not done that. To see the object as thought is not the same as seeing thought as object. One must find thought as object before thought can find itself in its object, that is, before thought sees the subject of the portrait. Nature, we may say again, is the portrait but not the subject, not the sitter, not the original.

What is called for is a situation that is both subject and object. In the theory of knowledge, these two must be distinguished. But they must also be identical. If only distinct, the problem has no solution and, as we saw above, no meaning.

There is one situation that unites subject and object. It is the functioning object, which is an object, but also a condition of objects.

A clear example is the yardstick. The yardstick organizes space. Without orderly space, nature is itself disorderly, and not nature but chaos. The yardstick is a piece of pine, but as pine it is only object. Pine does not order space. I don't know what a yardstick is made of. I have one in maple, others in steel, linen, plastic—and all are yardsticks. There is no chemistry of an object called a yardstick. I deny that one "perceives" a yardstick. I deny that one can ask, "How long is a yardstick? How much does it weigh? Where do you find them?" On the other hand, I deny that it is an item in the stream of consciousness, perhaps more clearly apprehended in a psychedelic haze induced by LSD or by transcendental meditation. I say, too, that space (or Space with a capital S) is the extension of functioning, the implication of the actual yardstick. *"Functioning object"* is an awkward term perhaps but the best I can do in familiar English.

Instead of "functioning object" one might speak of symbols or signs. But "symbol" suggests no continuity of itself and the "real" object. *The Farmers' Almanac* shows a table of symbols and signs for the zodiacal regions and for the planets. The astronomer, however, measures and calculates, and his description of objects occurs in terms of his functioning objects and therefore entails the verb and the act. The steersman goes by a compass, which is more than a psychological content of consciousness and is allied with the continuum through which he moves. Mathematicians and physicists got Armstrong and Aldrin to the moon. Those men were not "responding to the environment"; they were declaring it.

The defect of Kant's categories occurs in the assumption that they are properties of pure reason, that is, that they are laws of order, but of order without specific focus. Every category has a focus, such as a yardstick or a clock, a thermometer, balance, or voltmeter.

Words, too, are functioning objects—objects, but also vehicles of will and action. Berkeley was in error in supposing that the tree in the park occurred only as idea, as quality of sense. When Adam named the animals, he was doing something more than assigning arbitrary tags. One does not get clear on cows and horses until they have been named, and so perhaps confused, and eventually distinguished after much puzzlement and reasoning.

Nature as experience, that is, as object, sensation, perception, or order, is a myth. Nature is indefinable without the functioning object, the local and specific embodiment of order. Nature is itself a projection of those of its own constituents that are functioning objects. Destroy them, and nature falls into confusion. It reverts to consciousness, where subject and object are no longer distinct.

Knowledge is neither diadic nor monadic, but triadic. The functioning object is a mid-point at which subject and object meet. It alone gives objectivity to thought and subjectivity to the object. Thought joins object in one actuality. The functioning object becomes the incarnation of thought. It points toward objectivity and toward subjectivity.

The functioning object is the meeting place of reason and act, of essence and existence. In the abstract, it mediates between thought and object. In the specific and concrete, it mediates also between mind and mind.

The functioning object is communication. One escapes from subjectivity by finding the evidence of other subjects. The objective is another mind, because only there is one's own subjectivity revealed as one's own approach to the common world.

Idealism has harbored these solutions. They occur in Hegel (*The Phenomenology of Mind*) and in Royce (*The Problem of Christianity*). But they have not been given much notice.

The body itself has not been a great success as a locus of

the psychic in so far as it has been treated as the seat of thought. Nor yet has it fared better when viewed as "responding" to nature or to stimuli. That only draws it into nature, but gives it no role in defining nature. It is when the body acts that it becomes psychic. And this action is not solicited by nature, but by something in nature that is already touched by action. Thus, one learns to write by responding to something someone has written. There is no learning in response to objects. Science is learning of a pure sort because it is controlled by the general conditions of learning, that is, by functioning objects. Ordinary learning is controlled by pleasure and pain, that is, by subjectivity. But knowledge is learning controlled by the functioning objects through which the very region of nature secures definition and order. This is why books on psychology never succeed in defining knowledge. They define habit. This is why they do not define freedom.

Knowledge, as was said earlier, can seek only itself. It has no object not defined through itself. Yet it must have an object. The functioning object in its many forms stands as both object and thought. It demands inquiry. It is not a perception, nor is it the ordered perception of the absolute mind. It is an actuality, finite yet demanding endless application. It embodies the absolute modes of experience and also of reality. It defines the necessary, including the necessity of the accidental. For, as actual, it is itself caught in the accidental, bespeaking finitude and particularity.

3

Spectacle and Spectator

Ancient philosophy gave no cosmic status to the individual. Ontology led *away* from the individual. The Christian Church supplied a place for the individual, a cosmic status. "Not a sparrow falleth." That was the appeal. That the individual was an *absolute* could be demonstrated only as an individual appeared. This was Jesus. This is the "mystery" of the incarnation. This was the "scandal" to Greeks and the "stumbling block" to Jews. To this day we are looking for a way to give status to the individual. Why was it not settled by the Christian doctrine? Because the world remained independent of the individual. For *both* pagan and Christian, the scene in which man appeared was not of his making. Man was not "the measure."

As men looked at the world they saw nothing individual in it. But they did look. The more they looked, the more that world differed from what the Christians had said it was. Dante is today a museum piece. But in looking man saw himself as a spectator only. He told what he took himself to have *found*. The empirical temper has deep roots.

Every effort has been made to keep the spectator out of what he alleges to have found. He was not to find himself in the world that he described. Nor was he to find any other individual there. If you exclude yourself from the world, you will also exclude me. Nobody is to appear there. Nobody's individual world is the world.

All that depended on a view the spectator had of *himself*.

If the world was a spectacle, then man was a spectator. But he was not allowed, did not allow himself, to find a spectator in the spectacle.

How was it managed to keep the spectator out of the spectacle? This came about because the way of looking was itself nonindividual. The looking was done in nonpersonal terms, such as "how many, how far, after what interval of time, for what cause, apropos of what substance or objects?" The spectator looked, but his looking was done in terms he took to be nonindividual, not peculiar to him as an individual.

Was the spectator to be allowed even his way of looking? Could he look and keep out of the picture? Was not his *way* of looking itself an intrusion? As looking came into focus, it was said that the assumption that he tell *only* what he found would not support his way of looking. Those ways were not among the findings.

There remained, then, no way of *telling* what was found. Any telling had to be grammatical and logical. It appeared in terms of how many, how much, and so on. No such ways of telling were among the findings.

There had, however, been a good deal of telling before the status of the telling came to notice. That, of course, was unavoidable. Until a story has been told, no question of its claim to be an innocent report in which the telling played no part could be raised.

But we were not only spectators; we were also tellers of what we had found in the spectacle. That was the difficulty.

Even the claim that there were spectacle *and* spectator got no support from the findings. That distinction was *not among the findings.* It was a distinction made *only* in the telling.

This is a momentous disclosure and has so been regarded.

So long as the distinction was looked for apart from the telling, it has proved elusive. It is not a finding.

All findings were characterized by the *way* of finding and so by the way of telling. But that there was a finding *at all* was itself not discovered apart from a telling. Spectacle and spectator, the assumption of a finding, are *told* distinctions, not *found* distinctions.

The individual had no place in a world unless the spectacle disclosed his presence. This he was determined—in a moral sense—*not to permit*. He succeeded. No particular of the world he found was an individual. He had excluded that possibility by the way he went about looking. It is no surprise not to come upon Napoleon when one does one's looking in terms of numbers, spaces, and times, that is to say in terms of yardsticks, clocks, and balances. Within a world so found and described, there is no Napoleon.

But the looking went on. The spectacle enlarged. We came to the world as reported by physics and the "exact" sciences. It was a world because it was not a mess. It was orderly. It was infinite. Above all, it was the world man had found by his own looking. It was not the disorder of "primitive" magic, of boundless novelty where all things were full of gods. That was rejected. It was not the world of early Christianity or of Dante. There had been surprising and unwelcome changes.

This world of science was not a revelation to a passive spectator. To get that new world, he had to *reject* or to modify an older view. There was more to it than a bland announcement of a peculiar state of affairs, where no attempt was made to *discredit* former views, and no suggestion that such former views were *not* to receive full faith and credit—*all* views being merely reports made by neutral spectators, all made without guile and with no intrusion on the part of the observers.

Not at all. The scientific world carried a criticism of earlier views. Science claimed to go about its looking in the "right way." You looked through a telescope, for example. You dropped weighty objects from a height to see whether rates of momentum differed. You used a calculus to determine the orbit of the moon. That was the right way to become a spectator. We call it "scientific method." I intend no irreverence, but "No man cometh to nature but by me," said the man of method.

In the world so disclosed, there was no individual. But

for all that it was a world that man had found. Not all men had done so, but certain peculiar, perhaps dangerous and subversive men who could be named and even locked up, or forced to shut up.

At the same time, these men denied that they were personally and individually parties to the spectacle. Yet, what they had to say and to show was humanly said. The great world appeared as a consequence of man's endeavor. The world of science is no individual's world. Nor did it contain any individual in the spectacle. But it was man's world, discovered on his own resources. It was *not* a spectacle passively perceived and so no better than any other alleged spectacle.

It was excluded, however, to say, "There is the world," and nobody has had anything to do with saying that it is there or what it is like as an order of objects. Scientists are very sticky on that point. The world is what *they* say, not what Aristotle or St. Paul said. Yet they deny that as individuals they had anything to do with the world that they have so magnificently disclosed. They deny that the world is anybody's portrait. You won't find Newton in the motions of the moon. People who purport to tell about Newton do not speak about the moon. They say that he was a member of Cambridge University, and that he wrote books on theology—things like that, quite unscientific.

So, no individual as yet. But something called "man" has made his appearance. He appears in his rejection of earlier views and in the new world, which his positive methods have disclosed. That world is no longer a passive spectacle with which man has nothing to do. This is a radical change from classic views of spectator and spectacle, as well as from the Judaic and Christian view. Job "laid his hand on his mouth"; Newton spoke and "all was light."

What made the difference? It was not, I presume, superior sense organs. Nobody lays earlier confusions to poor eyesight or to defects in the medulla oblongata. Something had intervened between spectacle and spectator to make the later scientific world something more than a perception of the spectator and more, too, than a theory concocted in his private mind, assuming that such theorizing could occur with merely perceptual data. We are persuaded that the scientific world is the "real" world, not a phenomenon or a fantasy. It is not even quite plausible to regard one's acceptance of it as a case of social "conditioning," as of a doctrine transmitted by parents or special teachers, such as priests or rabbis who inculcate a particular creed. The world of science seems rather a "natural" world. Like good wine, it needs no bush. It cuts across the indoctrinated views of every sort. The moon landing was noted all over the earth. It was a scientific accomplishment accepted by all, strangely continuous with common faith even when its intricacies lay far beyond most persons' competence to understand.

These features—naturalness, universality, absence of indoctrination—led the great Kant to propose that the nature of things known included a nonempirical factor, a control in the spectator, or in his looking. The strength, or fitness, of this proposal was shown by the hostility that it aroused. It was close to the mark in so far as it accounted for the naturalness, universality, and authority of science. Perhaps it gave to science more authority than seemed compatible with the radical empiricism of many scientists who would prefer to forgo authority rather than be bound by an *a priori* order.

An objection to Kant, perhaps more felt than expressed, was his assigning to scientific knowledge and to the world so described a merely *phenomenal* status. Nature was not the "real" world. While clinging to a sort of empiricism, proposing to confine itself to what was *found,* and might *not* be found, and might be *otherwise* found, the scientific temper nevertheless wanted what it found to be "real." A pure empiricism, however, raises no question about "real" and "not-real." It has no basis for the question. It is not possible to give the status of "real" to what one happens upon. The real is usually regarded as enjoying its status *whether or not* it is perceived or noted by any spectator. "To be is to be perceived" has offended realists who nevertheless have also regarded themselves as empiricists. The real is to have a status apart from being perceived. Nothing is surely real until one can say of it that it is *not* being perceived. That view has been and continues to be a wide-spread and stubborn persuasion. In so far as the world of science is merely empirical, it cannot *also* be real. As gen-uine spectators making no pretension of having any hand in the spectacle, we are in no position to allege any status other than phenomenal to whatever the spectacle may pre-sent. The *ens realissimum* is not an empirical finding and never was.

So, if the world of science is to show the "real" world, and not the illusions of our prescientific ancestors, it requires a factor of which we say that it is *not* perceived. Without that factor, we are back to phenomena: to a mess, or to the regulated phenomena of Kant.

Scientists and their followers grant no reality to the arts, to history, to philosophy. The prescientific ages were dark ages. They had no reality. They had illusion and supersti-tion. Their world was a myth.

The question comes to this: What is there about the sci-entific world that endows it with a conviction of reality precisely because it is *not* perceived, is *not* a phenomenon, is *not* an empirical and accidental finding, is *not* an item in the spectacle, is *not* a prejudice of the spectator coloring and deforming what he empirically finds? Something familiar, surely, although not perceived.

This is the functioning and the "functioning object." In the case of physics, it is the yardstick, clock, balance, none of which is a "perceived" object analogous to sticks and stones. They are not "substances" like sodium or iron. Like the real, they do not get their status from being perceived. They must *not* be perceived if they are to be a factor in our assurance of the reality of the physical world. They meet that requirement. A yardstick is for measuring. Note the present active participle, the verb.

The terms "yardstick," "clock," and so on, are not common nouns. Genera and species do not apply. They fall into no "class" of objects in terms of the way of dis-criminating objects. They are not "mental" objects. Nor are they physical objects. Functioning precedes such dis-tinctions, permits them, enforces them, embodies them.

A functioning object leads to verbs, to a doing, to an

act. The great world of science results from action, not from the disengaged spectator of a spectacle.

The world of science is our achievement. That is a deep persuasion. It is the world of counting, calculating, measuring, inferring. It is wholly consequent upon functioning objects and their intimacy. Any functioning object is a command to do. A yardstick is nothing if not for measuring; a word is nothing if not for another word to be spoken; a clock, for telling time. Both the real and the apparent are projections of functioning.

This is not "response," so dear to psychologists. There is nothing specific to be done about a clock or about numbers or about the Parthenon. None of that has "relevance." Beware the person who asks about the relevance of mathematics or who calls it a tool. All that is an evasion of the actual, a retreat to a nonfunctioning oblivion. There is nothing to be done about the world disclosed through the functioning objects that generate physics. One does not "respond" to it; one maintains it. Although nature is no object, neither is it an illusion or an idea. It is the projection of actualities. It is not a theory. Nature looms as a vast presence because it is no less immediate than the functioning objects that embody its order. An object is real when it appears in terms of the order of appearances. It is fictitious or illusory when it does not so appear. The actual is the watershed of the distinction between the real and the illusory.

One needs to account for the deep persuasion that the world disclosed by physics is not a mere appearance. It is not real, but it contains whatever is real. It is not appearance but contains all appearances.

The real may not be merely another appearance; yet a reality that puts in *no* appearance meets with charges of nonsense. It seems plain, therefore, that we require appearance to claim a reality. It is odd that we should demand both that anything real put in an appearance and also claim that the real is something more than appearance. What more could it be? And where would we have come by the conviction that the real is more, or other, than appearance, while scoffing at those who propose a reality that does *not* appear and for that very reason seems to them to meet a basic demand of reality?

In my student days, the big controversy lay between idealism and realism. There was no middle ground. The defect of both was in a total ignoring of the actual. Neither party could find a place for the other. The realist would not settle for appearance and the idealist for a reality that was not an appearance.

The middle ground is the actual. This is the midworld. It is yardsticks, clocks, balances, words, utterances, monuments. It is on such terms that the real and the apparent are separated.

This basis of separation could not occur unless the functioning object *combined* appearance and reality. One sees a yardstick, one handles it. It is not outside the senses. Yet neither is it a "real" object, real because having a status without being perceived. This combination of authority and appearance occurs in the functioning object. It is the embodied order.

Idealism lacked an embodied order; realism lacked an apparent presence.

The basic functioning object is the body, not *a* body, but *the* body. The body is not an object among all other objects. How would one set about finding *the* body? It is an immediacy. It is the immediacy of function. Even the distinction of seeing and hearing depends on action. Why else associate red with green rather than with sounds, tastes, and pain?

Nature is unquestioned because it is the consequence of the control of all questions. It is the consequence of functioning. That is the locus of the act. Behaviorism posits nature but repudiates the functioning of which nature is the consequence. That is why it falls back on "response" but has no responsibility. But once you count fingers and toes, the mathematical fat is in the fire, and you come upon what must then be further said, amazing things like "zero" and "minus two dollars" and even transcendental numbers.

Although yardsticks and all other utterances are not

objects, neither are they isolated from objects. They announce the continuity of all objects with the functioning object. The yardstick is seen; it is handled; it is in a place. But it is also a factor in specifying the place where one keeps it. The body is the functioning center of all declared environment, yet it is not isolated but continuous with air, light, and the ground for walking. Functioning discovers its environment as it discovers itself. Neither is separable from the other. This is the sense of the authoritative immediacy of nature. It is as close as breathing and "nearer than hands and feet." What possible authority has nature otherwise? The record is clear: divorce nature and functioning, and each becomes a dogma and a mystery. The scientific world of the behaviorist is pure dogma, quite as much as his despised soul or mind.

Nature as arbitrary assumption is the other side of the arbitrary manager, precisely the objection made to the managing behaviorist. He is not responsible *for* nature or *to* nature. He misses the act because he has no functioning. All intimacy with nature is lost. It is not we who maintain it as the projection of doing. The verb is not constitutional for him. We forget, or have not seen, that nouns without verbs are miraculous and unaccountable. But, on the other side, verbs without nouns are equally mysterious. What was amiss in the creation story was not the use of verbs, but the absence of common nouns. Certainly there is no world until it is said. All the words of actuality must be spoken—this, that, there, here, now, then, yesterday, and tomorrow, and especially the negative "not." But every such universal also particularizes. In principle, the particular is also a universal and the vehicle of any universal is an utterance. The famous question of universals was insoluble so long as the verb had no constitutional place. It was supposed that particulars had no need of any doing, including utterance. They were not *"vox, praeterea nihil."* But universals might be. It was not seen that the particular was also a universal and that it was embodied in functioning and in utterance. "The Greeks had a word for it." That is why they launched the intelligible world.

In the functioning actuality, the act, the inherent control of the act, there, and nowhere else, is freedom. We are free *because* we assert nature. It is our world, as immediate as our breathing and looking or as our counting and measuring—all present active participles, all verbs. There is no world *within* which I breathe and speak.

The evidence of action is the very world now alleged to make action impossible. I have not looked for action within a prior world, but as the constitution of any world. The act becomes luminous as it has generated its own negation. "We are nearer to spring than we were in September, / I heard a bird sing in the dark of December."

And, after all, if one is to claim a constitutional place for action, it would be necessary that a state of affairs, in seeming opposition to act, be itself a consequent of doing. In this case, the opposition is made by science and the supposed physical world. The claims of action as constitutional could not be satisfied unless it had generated its own antagonist. That, of course, is a "dialectical" process, noted by Plato and made more explicit by Hegel. Nature is then neither a perceived object nor an illusion but a fatal aspect of the original and self-declarative act. If nature is not necessary in order to become aware of one's active presence then the act is not constitutional but another item of experience. But it has become clear that as an item of experience the act is elusive. Seeing, hearing, and so forth, lead to objects and to nature, not to action. The act must be the control that leads to nature and endows it with its authority or else it is not found.

Where what had been called an "act" becomes a locally "conditioned" response, there nature itself collapses into a nonrational concommitance of phenomena without any inherent order. It is notorious that all the modes of order in nature have been challenged and derided. This is only the other side of overlooking the present active participle even in so elemental an experience as seeing and hearing. A world without action is a world without form.

The human body, like other functioning objects, is no event in the impersonal order. As a yardstick is a piece of

wood but not as a unit of length, so too, the body is physical material, but not as the determiner of qualities (senses)
nor as a necessary element in the specification of abstract
modes of order, such as "place where." (Aristotle had
"space" and "place where" as categories.) The tree is
"green" because it is *seen* to be so; it is "15 feet away"
because one so determines by taking 5 steps of 3 feet each,
or by some other regulative measurement.

The functioning of the body is *cognitive.* Its very identification as *one's own* is a knowledge–situation. No body
can be one's own as a "matter of fact." It is so as a matter
of *act.* There is more than physics and chemistry in the
body because those orders depend on the body for their
modes of functioning, such as measuring spaces and telling
time, or counting, or using symbols. The body is the
occasion of such activity.

The body is *the absolute artifact,* that is, it is the artifact
that in its functioning creates all other artifacts and symbols. It is the absolute *actuality,* that is, the union of form
and content in functioning. It is neither abstract form nor
abstract content, this being a distinction that occurs apropos of its own activity.

All the ways of defining it are *reflective,* as when one calls
a body *the* body, that is, "one's own," an identification not
made in terms of any purely disembodied position. It is
"material," yet only to an activity that includes its own
participation. Its "physical properties" are named in terms
of modes of order necessitating artifactual symbols, must
be seen, or heard, or observed and handled. It is "mortal"
in terms of sequences requiring its own limited actuality
for the identification of a temporal transition, that is, of
specific transition, not of *any* change at *any* time.

To treat it as another object, that is, as material for one's
purposes, is to mistreat it. Just as the care of the body is
the most elementary love, so its disregard is most elementary barbarity. The moral defect of mistreating the body
of another derives from the place of the body as the actuality of the person, so long as the body can *function* as
actuality. The injury of the body is the denial of actuality

in principle. That is why health is basic. It is the reason for the *violent* reaction thought not improper when the body is attacked. It is thought proper that an attack on an idea be treated with forebearance. He who attacks an idea is already on the side of ideas. But violence to the body brooks no delay and courts a reply in its own terms.

4

Action and Order

Thunderstorms have had scientific and magical explanations. The experience is allegedly the same to the tribesman of Gabon and to the Harvard professor. The difference between them lies in the explanation. The professor denies that the storm is anyone's doing. The theory, however, is the professor's doing and may even have been baptized with his name. The data are neutral. How are they to be explained? Perhaps by Thor, Jove, or Henry Hudson and his merry men; perhaps as a result of electricity and the collision of air masses. The learned have no advantage in visual and auditory acuity, nor do they claim it.

A great point has been made of this neutrality of data to the perceiver, and of the perceiver to the data. The perceiver is like a wax tablet. He receives impressions will-he, nill-he. The more astonishing and the more inexplicable, the more neutral and reliable. Why he should then devise a "theory" about them, he being only a passive recipient, is not clear on the premises. Indeed, it has been characteristic of this account that the perceiver also possesses a mysterious faculty called his "reason," presumably quite independent of the data. Why this antecedent reason would trouble itself with those data remains equally mysterious. Why should not this reason continue to enjoy an agreeable independence, retaining its own purity and not meddling with impertinent data that arrive without leave, like intruders and troublemakers? One might advise reason to mind its own business and turn its back on this unreasonable rout of helter-skelter data. Those professors have been a meddlesome lot in forcing their reason on the data and the resultant theories on other people. Some have openly admitted that they propose to *impose* a logical pattern on the data, which, of course, they regard as needing discipline.

All my life I have been shy of the arbitrary and I have found that men of so-called reason are the most arbitrary of all. To begin with, I find it strange when the data get represented as foreign intruders or as magical apparitions, as a "given," which I could in no way associate with the recipient. The fact is that I was never without some intimacy with my eyes and ears, or with the taste of food, the sense of breathing easy or hard when I played "run sheep, run." I would say, too, that "my eyes ache" or "my tooth aches." As I take it, the intellectual professor wants me to treat all that as alien, as having no connection with me. "My eye," indeed! That possessive pronoun is an evidence of a primitive animism, like that of the tribesman of Gabon. The intellectual rule is: Never identify any data, or any object, with yourself, or yourself with any object. Dismiss all data, avoid all intimacy with objects, hold them all away, and devise a theory to explain the inexplicable. For it is plain that if these data and objects possessed some intimacy, and made sense to begin with, I would not be needing to stretch them on the Procrustean bed of Russell's logical postulates.

Now, it has become embarrassing to claim any direct identification with data and objects. Obviously, such claims do not have, and could not have, any defense. Man can't get outside the immediate and look it over, or think it over. It has no environment. Of course one could be led to argue that to allege an environment is to have employed some immediacy in its discovery and in its identification. I see no fault in that. But I would like something simpler and more affirmative.

What I propose is that nobody can claim to "see" unless he *looks,* and to "hear" unless he *listens*. He has to do something. Why do I say that red goes with blue, but not with sweet, or the sound of thunder? What associates qualities? Given blue, can I infer red or yellow? Qualities are discrete. You cannot say that I am color-blind because I now see no red. It is when I *look* and see no red that you make the judgment. But what goes on when I look? Why, I turn my head, or my eyes, shade them with my hand, move into a more favorable position. Then I say that I see blue or red. The perception has an intimacy. What, is it not just a mysterious datum, a given, an apparition? Is it not to be entertained tentatively? Is it not quite alien? I say it is not. The experience carries the authority and immediacy of my action. As sure as I stand here, I see the quality. "I would not this believe but for the sensible and true avouch of mine own eyes." But Hamlet had gone to the platform, put himself there, and looked, held his attention to seeing—a present active participle—not meanwhile fingering his sword to see if it was sharp or smooth, dismissing the rout of data in order to look. The avouch is not in a pale light, it is in the looking, in the act. The data have the *authority of the act* that permits their association as seen or heard. The alienation from data is the alienation from action; and that is the end of looking; and that is the end of seeing red or blue and of associating red with blue, rather than with thunder. The immediacy of quality is a factor in the immediacy of the act. The act is the warrant of the perception.

The trouble with Berkeley derives from his having no eyes. He never *looked*. But those who found fault with him had no eyes either. They argued only about the status of qualities and were as devoid of actuality as that exasperating bishop. They did anything but look.

This looking involves qualities and objects. Hamlet goes up to the battlements. He walks. He walks on stone steps. He is at one place, not anywhere else. He uses his legs, keeps his balance, wears clothes, carries a sword. All that is part of the immediacy that "avouches" what he then sees. He is not a total stranger, injected into a condition where he may be "given" a visual sensation. He has sensation *already,* and objects as well. All these objects had already been identified through action. One's own body is a functioning immediacy, not an object come upon by chance. This immediacy, to repeat, is functioning. There is no intellectual way of identifying one's own body, one's eyes and ears. The intellectual is likely to disapprove of statements when not about bodies—about ghosts, for example. But it would be hard to imagine any entity *less* embodied than alleged "data" or the "reason," which imposes its ways upon them, constructing theories. One cannot "postulate" looking, or any other actuality, treating functioning as an idea and then looking around to see if it had fitness or application.

So far as I know, there is no "postulate set" for original functioning like looking and listening. There are no rules for such activity. Suppose you say "To see, open your eyes." But I do not have eyes to open until I *have* seen and, what is more, looked. The actual is the original.

Suppose you go to the tribesman of Gabon with a writing as follows: "Postulate 2. If $a < b,$ then a and b are distinct." What does it mean? Well, it is said to mean that "if a precedes $b,$ then a and b are different." This is given as a postulate for a "simply ordered class or series." Notice the use of the present tense. What would the tribesman of Gabon, or you, or I for that matter, make of it where no past experience had taken place? Would he look, or would he listen? And how would he decide that simple question unless he had *already* discriminated in *action* between looking and listening? It is not without interest that no intellectual formula employs the past tense. "If $p \supset q,$ it does not follow that $q \supset p$" $(p \supset q \sim \supset q \supset p)$. Or, $S = \frac{1}{2}gt^2$. What has preceded? What follows? Logic applies to any object or event in so far as it enforces a connection with other objects or events. But it proposes no particular object. One counts sheep or men. Mathematicians won't have it that what they say depends on *having* seen a sheep, or on having seen anything in particular. But Hamlet finds avouch in the seeing and looking, he *having* moved to the platform, clothed and in his right mind. The curious consequence is that the intellectuals also insist on my looking. I am to "verify" my formula or hypothesis. In the extreme case, I may not know whether a whole formal sequence has an illustration or application.

For myself I find that very odd. Where does this idea of illustration or "application" come from? Why should any theory need to be "verified"? To what am I required to pay attention when that is demanded? By what authority am I asked to leave theory and go to the facts?

Many treat the atom as a hypothesis, as a "hypothetical entity." They say that if such an entity is assumed, their observed events can be put in order and be brought under control in a laboratory. The atom as hypothetical entity (1) makes observations intelligible (explains them) and (2) permits the control of experiment.

I think that the ordinary person is likely to see merit in the first of these two claims: atoms clarify or explain observation. This assumes that our observations are to be trusted. A hypothesis is *answerable* to such observation. The *observation* is the court of judgment. One has to consider that a hypothesis of that sort might *not* be sustained by observation. In that way one sees that the observation is the authority to which one refers the hypothesis. Observation *tests* the hypothesis. That seems sensible. A hypothesis needs a test.

On such assumptions the observations are themselves free from hypothesis in so far as they operate as the test. Something *not* hypothetical operates to accredit or discredit any hypothesis. If you estimate the area of a room and check with a yardstick, then the yardstick is not in question.

So, what is this "observation" that is to credit *or* discredit the hypothesis? Without hypothesis of any sort it is the stream of consciousness, nothing more.

But in terms of the stream of consciousness no question of credit or discredit can occur. Nothing in that stream can *raise* a question.

Yet the hypothesis implies that one *does* have a question. It says that something in the stream is obscure, puzzling, not accounted for. But on the premise that observation is the court of appeal, the locus of test, nothing there can be obscure. What is the sense of raising questions in terms of the very authority that is to decide all questions?

Observation, it seems, is to answer questions that it cannot so much as raise.

Hypothesis is the admission that the stream of consciousness is not clear. Yet in terms of that stream, no question so much as arises.

Why, then, project a hypothesis to explain observations that suggest no lack of clarity? And if observation does suggest such a lack of clarity, why appeal to it for a test? Are the blind to lead the blind?

So, we face the question of where the hypothesis comes from. It does not come from observations, from the content of the stream of consciousness. It is the hypothesis itself, and in principle, that is the wholly *unaccountable* element on the premises.

I would suggest that the popularity of the hypothetical, its flavor of broad-mindedness, is a consequence of its complete mystery, on the premises. Nobody can tell where he gets a hypothesis. It is a "free" idea. He cannot say that hypothesis is *forced* upon him by his observations, that observations are inherently rational, orderly, logical, structural, that they are *therefore* insecure on their own terms. A puzzling observation displays a structure. The planets wander; the other stars keep in orderly procession; why, then, do planets wander? In the interests of keeping order we then projected hypotheses about planets. What is observed is to fit into a scheme. Planets, as mere phenomena, threatened the assurance of our views about the stars. Why should not a star take to wandering as planets do? And if they could, why raise any question about planets? All could wander so far as observation alone could tell. No expectations can then hold, none would be so much as proposed. On the premises, nobody would be upset if stars took to wandering. The planetary appearances would pose no puzzle.

The interesting question, then, is where the hypothesis comes from, why it would be proposed, how it could be suggested. For, on the premises, observation is not itself puzzling. Rather, we appeal to it to answer puzzles. But why should we have puzzles at all when we are to fall back on an assured test for puzzles? Leave them alone and stay with an experience that *raises no questions.* Why not? This is exactly what the drug-culture recommends. You "expand" consciousness. You get rid of puzzles.

So, the statement "the atom is a hypothesis" becomes quite inexplicable. It is a wholly gratuitous idea, lawless in its origins, incapable of being tested by an experience that is only what it happens to be. As I suggest, the popularity of hypothesis among intellectuals derives from this lack of enforcement. Propose a hypothesis and you seem to stand in the clear, not constrained in its projection, let alone its test.

One could operate here by focusing on the method of test. But while that would be just as good an approach I am working it from the other end, asking rather what could *propose* a hypothesis. I say, then, that the stream of consciousness, the psychological, raises no questions whatsoever, and that it cannot be appealed to for a test of an utterly indefinable problem, indefinable on the premises.

In any matter-of-fact statement or belief, we commonly recognize contingency and feel gratified when a belief can be supported by evidence. It is not too much to say that a belief is what the evidence suggests or requires. A belief without evidence or reason is not so much arbitrary as it is incomprehensible. No belief appears as an unconnected conviction unrelated to prior experience. There has been loose talk about the "hypothesis" as if it were a miraculously conceived guess that subsequent evidence confirms or falsifies. Where the alleged data are discrete and unconnected, no hypothesis can be suggested. I have heard bland proposals of some hypothesis from speakers who posed as open-minded empiricists recommending themselves as superior to any arbitrary or dogmatic prejudice. They smile and say that, of course, their proposal is "only a hypothesis." One is left gaping at such an unaccountable apparition, a bolt from the blue, in no way consequent upon any prior experience or requirement. A hypothesis not itself a requirement—and appealing to data, themselves equally miraculous and discrete—can find neither confirmation nor falsification in that formless medley. This is nihilism in disguise. In terms of radical empiricism, a hypothesis is an unaccountable miracle, quite as much so as the miraculous data that are to test it. There is no test of miracles, and no connection among miracles. Where requirement is dogma, a test is nonsense. But that is the pose of the intellectual. He flatters me by proposing a test and then calls me a dogmatist if I claim the authority of testing. Even any assurance that I, a person, am there to hear his words is regarded as an unwarranted superstition, as, indeed, it is on his premises. If enforcement be dogma, then hypothesis is nonsense—miraculous in origin and impotent in result.

Since the search for the facts sends me to data, the merely given, I am at a loss to understand what that disorderly rout of qualities could possibly offer by way of confirmation or rejection. Is order, that is, theory, to appeal to *disorder* for its truth? It seems implausible. On the premises it makes no sense.

The experience that I am bidden to consult sends me back to simplicities and to immediacies. But are they shapeless? Not if they are such as looking and listening. Then I fall back on the sensible and true avouch of eyes and ears. I am back to personal pronouns, to action, to control, and to the whole state of affairs allied to the looking and listening. I cannot be sent to the facts unless I have *never left* the scene of action with all its furniture and functioning. Where no actuality has been assumed, no theory could be verified. Without the actual, empiricism is a vagrant. It is notable that when the variety of data appeared to rob us of all assurance and of all control, we have fallen back on what we can *do,* namely count, utter numbers, draw lines and figures. Whatever reliable order was invoked by Descartes, and seen by Hume, was of that sort. For anyone who utters numbers or draws lines mathematics becomes curiously authoritative. And if I speak I learn that I can't have cake and eat it too. The authority of all form is that of the act or, as people say, of an operation. The authority of form and content has the *same warrant*. The avouch in both cases is in the immediacy of the actual whether that be the looking or the utterance of numbers.

The link between form and content is the act that entails both. Otherwise the mathematical ideal of Descartes and of many others is as disembodied as Hamlet's father's ghost. It is curious to consider how persistently we have disavowed the functioning actuality of looking, listening, counting, and measuring. The so-called exact sciences get represented as exact about *objects* rather than as simply in the act itself, its immediacy and momentum. The avouch of one's eyes is no less authoritative than that of any other controlled and self-identifying operation. The pure spirit cannot count, measure, weigh, or tell time.

Scientific explanations are the advance line, but logistics have to be maintained with the rear if we are not to arrest the advance because of a lack of supply. The tribesman of Gabon is not wrong to see the world as actual, rather than as theoretical. The only possible order is that of the act. There is the sole locus of control. There is the corrective nemesis, whether one looks or counts. The tribesman interprets all events and objects in terms of action, his immediacy. Children do this. They ask why grass is green, as if some purpose were thereby accomplished. St. Francis spoke of brother fire and sister water. The stars in their courses fought against Sisera. Control begins as personal. To ask the tribesman to interpret thunder impersonally is to rob him of the very source of his own acquaintance with all objects. They stand in relation to his acts. They are viewed as controlled as he is also controlled, and have ascribed to them the same cause of action. Thirty years ago a physicist was talking sociably about the Wilson cloud-chamber. Particles of smoke dart about when an electric current is run through the chamber. He said to us, "They behave almost as if they were alive." In the absence of a formula he fell back on animism.

How, then, is one to understand the emergence of the impersonality of science? It has long struck me that the famous Seven Liberal Arts all had to do with utterance and so with local control. Grammar was control of speaking, arithmetic of counting and calculating, geometry of finding distances and places. These arts were "liberal," that is, free, that is, not the area of helplessness. Peter Damiani laments that some monks apply themselves to the Rule of Donatus rather than to the Rule of St. Benedict. The liberal arts are the loci of action and of controlled action. They are not direct "responses" to accidental "stimuli." They were cultivated by the free man.

I note that all the arts and sciences function through the functioning artifact. The "facts" become resultants of such symbolic control. I would not this believe but for the avouch of my own logic, of my own calculation. The impersonal world of science is the resultant of a local and artifactual control. Even the tribesman of Gabon does some counting. He has a few words and knows that "here" is not "there." He can see and also hear, and the two differ. He knows that one place is farther than another, takes longer to reach afoot. There lurks the origin of the scientific impersonality. Action itself entails universal factors: how many, how much, how far, how heavy, how hard, how different. Science emerged with the control of those immediate factors of action. Thales could tell how far off from the harbor a ship stood at Miletus. He had some geometry and thought it a wonder, a marvelous power.

A yardstick does not behave as if it were almost alive but short of operating with it there is no way of rescuing it from the condition of a piece of wood. I am there, I use it. The consequences are considerable. I discover infinities, extensive and intensive. The vast impersonal looms.

Now the "intellectual" is the man who has forgotten his logistics, has no source of supply to the rear, and so has cut himself off from action. "Act" has become a naughty three-letter word. If you are not careful, you will fancy that you behave as if you were almost alive.

I restate the chief consideration: Both quality and impersonal form assume the actual. They assume some state of affairs that is itself specified by functioning. There is no state of affairs such as Hamlet on the platform, or the astronomer in the observatory, if functioning has established no discrimination and no order. There is a residual animism. We join the tribesman of Gabon.

Now it is a consequence of scientific order that the thunder be not attributed to Thor or Jehovah. What scientism overlooks is that this very denial draws its force from the *activities* that control the identification of qualities, of spaces and causes.

The order that contests against magic in nature is *the order of action,* and the role of action is the identification of both content and form. This is the point that scientism has overlooked. And because of this obscurity in its own articulation, it has lost contact with the tribesman of Gabon and can only tell him that he is wrong and superstitious. The scientist has no way of enforcing his own point of view if he cavalierly dismisses looking and listening, counting and measuring, as constitutional factors in his own inquiry and in his own results.

One has to go far back and challenge the possibility of a nonactive experience. That is what the above considerations attempt to do. Make sense without doing, and my argument has failed. There is the issue. I propose the order of finitude as a category. That is the actual.

5

Philosophy Is Just Talk

Philosophy is just talk; its distinctive words and their order have *no denotation*. Critics have succeeded in removing philosophical terms from the "control of consciousness"— soul, mind, matter, necessity, and so on. Berkeley's denial of "matter" is not peculiar, only more arresting, and its lack of acceptance by common sense shows that common sense has a deep attachment to talking "about" something to which talk is directed. Matter seems to make talk "about" possible. But what one talks about need not be "matter"; it could be a spirit—the soul, ghosts, a deity. Such objects have also been attacked as no content of consciousness.

What we talk "about" is not, it seems, defined by the talk. We could talk or not without changing or affecting what we refer to in our talk. This has seemed an essential feature of talk "about." Anything talked about goes its own way, talk or no talk.

Even the content of consciousness gets talked about, as if its being noted by speech had nothing to do with its occurrence. But "content of consciousness" has met the same critical fate as Berkeley's "matter." "Consciousness" is not itself in the stream of consciousness, any more than is matter or the soul, or causality.

The result has been that the common-sense insistence that talk be "about" something not defined in the talk, with a status unaffected by talk—that this insistence has been discredited. Nothing talked "about" can be captured in the

talk. No one can exhibit *in talk* what he is talking about,
not matter, mind, soul, or the moon. We can give no
account of what it is that we talk about. A man cannot say
"I know what I am talking about" and expect to be cred-
ited in so far as what he claims to *know* has that separation
from whatever he may say about it that talking "about" it
requires.

The statement "I know what I am talking about" is met
with skeptical reserve. Someone else may say that he does
not know what I am talking about. Berkeley said that, as
for himself, he did not know what others were talking about
when they spoke of matter or of cause. Hume, of course,
made a more explicit denial of cause and of those "necessary connections" that so many had been talking "about."

Some access to what one is talking about is required.
What is that mode of access? Who admits that I have it?
Can I expect an audience if I say "You may not like my
words, but just the same I know what I am talking about"?
I would get set down as a dogmatist or as an unreasonable
fellow. I would be claiming that whatever sense you could
find in my words I know what I am talking about. I would
not, of course, blame you for not knowing what I know.
Each would be "entitled" to his own knowledge and his
own talk about it. You might, of course, soon tire of my
talk since you were not yourself directly acquainted with
what I was talking about. But you could not allege that my
talk was foolish. Your not knowing what I was talking
about would disqualify you from alleging any lack of sense
or truth in what I was saying. No hard feelings either way.

It seems worth noting that we often associate for just
talk, enjoying remarks and stories, talk for its own sake.
There is something of this in mathematics, where we go
on talking in mathematical terms, not raising questions
about the numbers, zero, infinity, not asking what in the
world a man thinks he is talking "about" when he speaks
of negative numbers or irrationals. What was Homer talking about? About Zeus or the grey-eyed Athena? But you
can't talk about such persons as if they and their ways had
a status quite apart from the talk. They are myths, unreal-

ities, not possibly independent of anything said about them. Nobody "knows" anything about Zeus. One cannot talk about Zeus. Sober and emancipated people patronize such talk. In history it is not evident what one is talking about where, as on the premises, one is to have knowledge of, or acquaintance with Plato, the polis, or the French Revolution as things, or objects, or realities quite apart from anything said "about" them. It would be hard to say "Let's talk about logic," where nothing said now or ever before exhibited or defined what one claimed to be talking about. And it has been claimed that logical talk is *not* about that nonlinguistic thing, object, or region "about" which we talk. In fact, it is claimed that logical talk is *bad* talk. James and Skinner want no part of it. The real is not logical.

It appears, then, that much talk is not "about" a prior state of affairs known quite apart from a saying. It appears that such mere talk is enjoyed, valued, and, in the case of math, given great authority. Chartres and the Parthenon are just talk, utterances that are enjoyed, sometimes viewed as revelatory, as Keats said of Chapman's Homer.

We face a condition where it has become hazardous to claim that one talks "about" anything at all. One is laughed at for venturing to say what one is talking about. The tables are turned. So, now we have lots of talking where anyone who claims to "know" what he is talking about is denounced as a dogmatist or metaphysician. Nobody can "know" what that may be which he then proposes to talk about. It is a curious reversal of common sense. But it was in the cards. The demand that we talk "about" what is in no way defined by talk, what goes its own way *whatever* we say, or *whether* we say anything at all, has backfired and left it impossible to give any account of what we talk about.

What, then, is the status of talk? On the premises that what we talk about is not defined by its being talked about, we would have to find talk itself as another alleged *object*. This object, or state of affairs, or reality, or thing—I don't know what to call it—would be as separate from talk as any other when it happened to be talked about. And since criticism has alleged that many such things talked about were not real—matter, cause, soul, and so on—it is not to be taken for granted that we could talk *about talk*. Indeed, what we ordinarily call talk has kept bad company. It is associated with persons, minds, souls, truth, falsity, other minds, usually with a purpose, a seeking for an end, a value. All that is very bad. For those are *precisely* the associations that have been most severely attacked as illusion. So it is not at all plain and clear that talk is something to be talked about. It may fade away like Berkeley's "matter" or Hume's "necessary connections" or "innate ideas" in Locke.

One must consider, too, that talk as commonly imagined has peculiar properties. For example, there are exclamations and questions, and these seem rather unlike ordinary objects, like swans or the moon. There are moods and tenses. In what way is one to come upon the subjunctive or imperative mood as an object about which we then talk? The usual properties of objects—color, odor, place, size, velocity—seem not to disclose a mood, let alone a subjunctive. The classic "categories" name properties that do not apply to a sentence containing "not" or "if," or to a sentence involving a past or future tense. But where else is one to look for a past or future, a negation, a hypothesis? How am I to talk about so elusive an object, or reality, as the past? Yet, if one is to talk "about" talk there must be, on the premises, a state of affairs in no way affected by its being talked about. Whatever a question may be it is not to be found in what we say, no more than we suppose that the maple tree in my yard requires talk in order to be the occasion of talk.

A sensible man who talks about ordinary objects—sticks, stones, the color of the moon when just appearing over the top of the hills—would, I believe, have some difficulty talking about the subjunctive mood on the same basis of observation or perception. Nor does the scientist peering through microscope or telescope come upon such items about which he then talks.

It very much looks as if talk were an illusion, in the same way as Berkeley's matter or Hume's necessary connections. As something to talk about in the usual way, talk seems elusive or even an absurdity.

Common sense does not treat talk as similar to objects talked about. The response to what someone says is made in the same medium as the provoking word. One *word* leads to another *word,* but the moon does not provoke another satellite of earth. One does say "Speak louder, please" and in that request one treats talk as an object to be perceived. Or, one might draw a chair closer to the speaker, or closer to a person hard of hearing. But in responding to what is said, the objective properties of a voice or visual medium are not operative. One notices that a speaker lisps or is hoarse or has a local accent, qualities that are ignored in a reply. It seems no part of common sense to deal with utterances as one does with a downpour of rain. The reply to what one takes to be an object is not a word, as Canute discovered. Nor can one reply to a word as if it were another object, making an appearance in the order of objects, accounted for in that order.

But the view that in terms of objects talk is an illusion seems entirely proper. This, I take it, is the conclusion reached by the scientific operator. Why not join him? There is then no such event as talk "about" objects. For the objects go their own way whether or not there is talk. Confining one's attention to objects, one comes upon no talk in the region of objects, among rocks or stars or protoplasm, in test tubes or telescopes. Talk is one of those illusions, a non-entity, nowhere observable, like matter, soul, or necessary connections.

For my part I agree with this claim that talk is not to be found. I join in it. Talk is not another item of common experience, like maple trees and oak trees, like red or some other color. It is not an empirically discovered event. In this it is analogous to matter or the soul or necessary connection, or plain connection. Give the behaviorist this point, and welcome. He is not to be refuted by the claim that one *does* find talk as well as pigeons or trees. One does not. I join in that insistence. I find no talk among objects.

Here is, then, the radical issue. For the claim that one does not find talk among objects seems to assume that one finds objects without talk. This I deny.

The reason why one does not find talk among objects is

the *same* as the reason why one does not find cause, persons, space, time, or logic among objects. Nothing pervasive, constitutional, structural, or universal is found among objects.

Unless utterance be a present in the discovery of objects, no objection to the behaviorist is possible. Unless utterance is a universal, it is an illusion.

Ask any man to show you a universal—cause, "this," "the," personal pronoun—and you embarrass him. He keeps talking in such ways, but has no defense. And should one not have a defense? Is one not to account for one's utterance of a personal pronoun, the definite article, matter, mind, value, fallacy? Must not the "intellectual" be prepared to account for what he says, the words he uses?

We resist the unconditioned. It seems obscurantist not to require an accounting for any word used, for speech itself in so far as it is an item come upon. But I am rejecting the assumption that I come upon utterance. I say it is *unconditioned*. It is rather the self-conditioning. No object is identified without a name. The word "object" is itself a word. Without the word no one perceives an object. Object is a status within a discourse. It is itself one of those baffling words and has given rise to a radical mistrust or radical confusion, as when one alleges a difference between subject and object, or between object and illusion, between a real and fictitious object. People balk. They say one is dealing in "metaphysics," raising dust, dealing only in words.

I grasp the nettle. Yes, one is dealing only in words. But I am not allowing *any* object without the word "object." Nor do I allow "I see a maple tree," where there is no word, including the word "not"-oak.

I want an *unconditional surrender*. But this surrender is to the presumption of conditioning, to that immediacy within which, and out of which, all conditional statements appear. "Where" has surrendered to the order of space. This order is in utterance, ultimately in a yardstick, which is *not* a perceived object nor so identified, not a content of consciousness, but a functioning object, like a word or *the* body, never found, but a premise of all findings, of all data, which are not discrete miracles.

Utterance is constitutional. I am not open to the claim that I have stumbled upon utterance when I might not have done so had I lived in Ireland or Israel.

Utterance is the actual. Every universal is a form of actuality, of doing, as space is of using a yardstick, or time of telling it by a clock, or cause by producing or preventing—present active participles. The present active participle has been overlooked by philosophers. In terms of *nouns* all organization words, all universals, have fallen into disrepute. Why should James deny logic? But why not, if utterance be only a phenomenon? On that premise there is no basis for any authority in logic. Civilization means utterance and its formal order.

To see utterance as unconditioned and constitutional is to make *all* action constitutional. Act apart from utterance has proved elusive. It does not turn up among the "facts." The categories are the basic acts. They are verbal. They require present active participles.

Nature itself is then a consequence of formal action. This is essential if the behaviorist is to be met. Give him objects or nature *without* action, without utterance, without *presence,* without present active participles, and then no way of escaping from his staccato account of behavior is available. Let speech or action be an empirically discovered event and one can say goodbye to logic and to ethics, to history and civilization, to energy and its inherent discipline.

6

"Explaining" Language

There has been a strong presumption that speech is to be *derived* from a state of affairs where there was *no* utterance. Of course *any* identifiable object, or what is taken to be an object, needs to be "explained" or accounted for—or so it is said. The exception is God, or whatever eludes the status of identifiable object. And of God, or any such *unenvironed* object, it is said that all passes into mystery at last, or that the ways of God are "past finding out," or are inscrutable.

The consequence has been to require the rationalist to speak *only* of objects. Without objects, no explanations; and rationalism offers the clarity of explanation in contrast to disorder, chaos, miracle, or mystery. The rationalist does not like the ineffable, what cannot be spoken about, made articulate, and so part of an order. All that is background to the consideration of the unenvironed. People speak of the "original." They wish to be "original" or "creative," not accounted for in terms of a prior order or state of affairs. Nobody is quite pleased when he is "explained." He feels nullified. At the same time, he may insist that any identifiable object, or event, requires explanation, that is, derivation from its environment.

Of course one may then observe to the person claiming to be original or creative that he is *not an object,* that an act is not an event *among* events. Such is the price of originality. But that consideration seems baffling and rationally unacceptable. Nor, in fact, does anyone wish to be quite unaccountable. The original person wishes to be recognized, perhaps even paid for his idea, song, book. He wishes to acquire a place in history, not merely to flash into oblivion. If so, he has appealed to some continuity common to all. Only apropos of such a continuity can his originality be understood, or be made memorable.

In any case, the unenvironed, whether God, nature, or the original act, has made trouble. It baffles explanation. And we tend to insist on explanation, that is, to make an object of every noun, including proper names, and so to place them in an environment that accounts for their appearance. It is generally considered sensible to ask, What are you talking about? When one can't say, one is accused of nonsense. Or it is asked, Why do you make that point? Or, Why do you bring that up? That anyone just talks, or acts, seems to convict him of irresponsibility.

The wide acceptance of behaviorism, of stimulus-response explanations of what had passed for acts, of "adjustment to the environment" shows the willingness to see word and act as *resultants* of an assumed environment. An infusion of grace, the seductions of Satan, or muscles, tendons, joints, and ductless glands affected by stimuli account for what I do or say. If "I" speak English, or count, or calculate, or love Mary, the question then becomes, What accounts for "your" doing thus and so? For, "He might have been a Roossian, a French or Turk or Proossian, or perhaps Italian. . . ."

But the going is not quite easy. Mathematicians do not like to admit a prior experience of numerically distinguished objects as the *a priori* environment of counting. No, math is "pure." It has nothing to do with apples or figs. So, the question "What are you talking about?" is an embarrassment to them. They deny that they are talking "about" anything in particular. Now, I am a philosopher, and people ask "What is philosophy about?" and I say "Oh, about nothing in particular," and they say "That is what I suspected." Neither mathematicians nor philosophers seem to be talking about what is "there."

Neither can so much as take refuge in illusion. They do

not even talk "about" what might be there but is *not* there, like Santa Claus, who lives at the North Pole and drives reindeer, which have names. So it comes to this: "There *you* are, and you speak English; therefore explain the circumstances that had on you the effect of saying 'one, two, three.' " It was said of Frost that he was asked, "Would you tell us just what you meant when you wrote 'Something there is that does not love a wall.' Tell us in good plain English, but not in poetry." Analogously to the mathematician, "Tell us just what you are saying when you count, in good plain English, since we do not understand mathematics." Did not mathematics, poetry, philosophy make their appearance in a state of affairs where no mathematics, poetry, or philosophy, no speech, no utterances had existed? Well then, in terms of that prior state of affairs tell us how numbers, music, philosophy happened to appear. For they must have *happened,* since a prior state of affairs can explain or account for them, or should be able to. And when this account is given, please to remember that I am no mathematician, poet, or philosopher, so please do not use these derivative utterances in your explanation. Only if you avoid such terms in your explanation would I be able to understand you. It is not fair for you who are a mathematician to insist on talking your way. Talk *my* way, remembering that I neither know anything about mathematics (or philosophy) nor care to study that special subject. I am a plain man but nevertheless I would, as a matter of scientific curiosity—a weakness of mine—like you to tell me what caused you to speak at all, or to speak like a mathematician or philosopher. Surely, there is some peculiar circumstance that influenced you to count or to sing. All I ask is that you make those circumstances plain to me, surely a reasonable request, rational, scientific.

Yes, and not only that. Here I am attempting some control of myself and also of nature. Therefore, I must find out why it is that I speak a *specific* language or sometimes find myself counting my money, or saying that I live 5 miles from North Adams. I am not in charge of myself if I speak in a specific language when I might speak in another or *none at all.* If there is "no royal road" to geometry, why pay attention to its plebeian ways? Why should Euclid be considered so smart when what he said was only a nasty crack at Ptolemy? He was, obviously, just an anti-monarchist. Let him have his plebeian geometry and have him watched by the secret police. Obviously, a troublemaker, a fellow who does not know his place. Impious too, when the marks he makes on a papyrus prove so fascinating and lead to a neglect of Jupiter Ammon. An idolater, if the truth be told, alleging that he can read off the shape of the whole world from some concocted lines on a piece of paper. Indeed, there is an element of magic in these mathematicians.

They do not say, of course, "Let there be a triangle" and thereupon a triangle appears *ex nihilo.* That is a divine or priestly magic. But they do "produce" a triangle, or even a line. And the odd feature of a line occurs in the *identity of the production and the observation.* A line requires a controlled production from terminal to terminal. A "straight line" satisfies a recipe, a rule, an act performed *according to rule.* A circle derives from a procedure; you keep your distance from a point called the center. Nor is there any such point without the procedure—as if, looking around, one were to say "Here is a center, and over there I see two more, but to the left none is to be perceived." One does not find centers as a squirrel finds acorns. The magic of geometry is the magic of action, where the act and the product are inseparable. The act is a living act, the word a living word. By such procedures a world is projected. Utterances make magic. Poets used to be regarded as "inspired," as were also storytellers. They wove a spell and kept children from their play and old men from the chimney corner. It is always destructive of the living word to ask what it is "about." It is either magic, or else a poor substitute for journalism and psychology. So, one cannot say what numbers and geometry are "about," or what Homer is "about," as if one already had met wrath and Achilles and had then, very cleverly, put one's information into hexameters. Clever chap, Homer.

It is notorious that "point" is not the name of an "object." It is not red, white, or blue, or somewhere, or of a specific gravity. But neither is "zero," nor the word "not" and a great many others—if, then, therefore, equal, necessary, identity, difference, part, whole. These words occur only in their utterance. All are formal; none denotative; none "about" an object, or a prior state of affairs. One cannot talk "about" such words as if they were objects, as if they accidentally turned up in a world I never made. All such words occur only in the act that produces them. For that reason there was no royal road. To command spatial order, one must "do" geometry. The person, the utterance, and the world become inseparable.

Before Homer smote his lyre, there had been words and symbols. Every word has some magic in it. Magic is a control. Utterance and control are inseparable, and there is no control until the symbol becomes a factor in action. The word is essential to the object. What does one see while walking in woods, if one does not know the names of trees, bushes, flowers, ferns, lichens? One sees only a blur. The object appeared when the Greeks had a name for it. The object is not "perceived" until there has been uttered an artifactual guide and control. That there *are* objects *is* the magic. It is curious that we take it for granted that the maple tree appears as a distinctive object. We say that we "perceive" it. Yet no maple tree is perceived except as it is *not* an oak. What conveys the negative, the exclusion, the difference? One *sees* no "not," no "not-oak." The abstract aether-wave tells nothing of the air-waves when it, allegedly, serves as "stimulus." Yet the maple tree, except as *not*-some-other-sort-of-tree, is no maple tree. The *vehicle of the distinction,* that is of the maple tree as a peculiar object, is the name and the negative.

There are no negatives among the objects, but there are no objects without the negative. The negative is made manifest only in the utterance. An object, as *this* one, not *that* one, requires *the vehicle that articulates the difference.*

If a man cannot "tell" the difference between maple and oak, one suspects that he does not perceive it. If the shep-

herd cannot tell his tale under the hawthorn in the dale, we
say that he cannot count, that he cannot *tell* the difference
between eleven sheep and a dozen. It isn't that he needs
eyeglasses; he needs to do counting.

"Object" is not itself an "object." "Object" is like
"point," or "zero." It is a universal, a formality, a term of
procedure, of functioning, of order. "Object" is not the
label pasted on a particular thing. So there is a fair question: What is the *vehicle* in which the particular experience
acquires the *status* of "object"? I answer that this vehicle is
utterance. No utterance, then no basis for the status of object.
What is more, no utterance, then no basis for the distinction of particulars, no *this,* which is *not that*. Words like
"this," "not," "that" are all significant only as they are
spoken, just as a line has to be produced and not passively
perceived.

We say commonly that if a difference cannot be "told"
there is no reason to believe that it has been "perceived."
On the other side, we cling to the view that the object was
"perceived" quite apart from any articulation of its identity
and difference. And we are strongly satisfied that the object
exists prior to its having been identified in a discourse. So
we say, "Why, *there is* space, time, quantity, peculiarity,
difference, this, and that—how, then, did we *come* to speak
of them?" It seems a fair question. My claim is that the
question assumes the region of objects, which has already
been made articulate, that the question itself embraces the
very region that is to account for the question. The question appears to be "about" nature and speech, as if both
could be talked "about" in the absence of their having been
identified in talk. You can't talk "about" talk; you can't see
your eye as object, where no seeing eye does the seeing.

Action and a world are inseparable. The word, symbol,
artifact focus the actual world. The expansion of the
immediate occurs *via* what has been done. We move from
that focus. The "stimulus," abstract and irrelevant, leads
to no expansion. The object, which already embodies act,
is the vehicle of further action. Because it embodies action
it contains the conditions of action. The stone used as a

hammer proposes hammering and its circumstances. That stone is no longer merely "a" stone, an object, a passing stimulus. It is an object, but now defined through function, not through color or touch. A yardstick is also an object, but it may be of pine, maple, linen, plastic, rigid steel, flexible steel, or of any substance. Common sense then alleges that one is wandering. Is a yardstick maple or steel? If you can't say, you are talking nonsense. What is its chemistry, how long is it, what does it weigh? If you can't tell, you are charged with dream or fantasy. The yardstick, however, is a *functioning* object. It is tied to action, to doing. And on that *doing* depends the whole vision of space and of its infinity. Nor is it a "tool" to be used for a purpose and then cast aside, as if one could now do without it. Such functioning artifacts *define the environment* but are not objects in a prior environment.

So, too, the stone used as a hammer. It serves as a means of exploration. What can it crack? Like the eye and ear it becomes not an instrument of a prior environment, but a factor of further exploration. My stone shows what I can do. It shows what *other* objects may be with respect to hardness. It proclaims other objects because it is more than an object. It is an object that defines other objects in terms of action and function.

As for articulate speech, as with the stone, the act and the occasion are inseparable. Words mark an occasion of action. Dictionaries illustrate the occasion. The word has no meaning apart from occasion. There is no "right" use of a word apart from actual discourse.

But we say that we were once like the animals, which have no language, no artifactual objects that command attention and enforce a continuing activity. The functioning object commands notice even when not in use. Numbers become themselves interesting when one is not counting sheep or money. No animal is a mathematician or grammarian, poet or scientist. And, happily, none is a philosopher. "I think I could go and live with the animals / they are so placid and self-contained. . . ." No animal is stupid. All have made adjustment to "the" environment.

From animal to man is from stimulus to artifact, from response to action, from momentary to continuous. Any continuum names an action, rather, a *way* of acting, not an object. Line, square, circle, zero, infinity, an individual, history—all these are *actual, not factual*. All are immediacies of action. All define a present perpetuating itself in a sequel.

The continuum is also the same as mind, or a world. It is always formal, that is, a *way*. Any "world" is a formality. Dogma, which deals in "realities," has never offered an authoritative immediacy and has always been hostile to the formal actuality, to words, which are elements in a self-modifying continuum. The defect in Platonism occurs in that words like "form" or "universal" are not themselves patterns fixed in heaven but are modified in the discourse that has launched them. Animals lack continuity, that is, mind or world. They have no artifacts of their own that are also commands. Mathematics is not a popular major. It deals in commands. It enforces attention and inquiry. If one says "zero" or "minus two" or "prime number," one has proposed further problems. One is no longer adjusting to "the" environment or confronting a world one never made. Popular studies are those that serve a purpose and flatter desires. All formality thereupon becomes an impediment, and we rail at the "Establishment" as if it, too, represented only desires, not the continuum of action.

We say that there are animals. But animals do not say so. That is why we see them as responding to "stimuli," accidental or devised. Animals did not aim at becoming persons. No, nothing of that sort happened. Well, what did happen? What was the *prior state of affairs* that "explains" the shift from response to act?

Now, there is the trap. Explanation has indeed been offered. After the animals, man was made. He, however, had a "soul." That was not his doing. It was a celestial arrangement, in the end inexplicable, past finding out.

Animals did not have a plan to become man. Besides, it has been held that no rational being would want to become human. Every prospect pleases, and only man is vile. Certainly, if there was a plan, the resultant product has not been satisfactory. But if, abandoning plan, one falls back on miracle and an imparted soul, one has not done any "explaining," least of all in terms of that prior state of affairs called nature.

I find these arguments tedious. That they have any propriety is a consequence of the objectification of utterance, of man, of nature, and of the supernatural. But I can make no object of nature, or of utterance, or of myself, or of another person. Indeed, all these distinctions are immediate and linguistic. They occur functionally, not in passive perception, not as accidents but as structure. I would say this: Show me utterance as one object among others, and I will look for an "explanation" of it in terms of the order of objects. That seems fair. But I do not find utterances as another object. Nor do I find "objects," the status of object, as another object any more than I find zeros or centers of circles or the square root of minus two or mistakes or crimes. There is no object without a word for object. It comes to that.

Consequently I am driven by the terms of the question to look for the origin of language in act and in functioning. I am looking for the emergence of the *functioning object,* not of the perceptual object. This functioning object does not appear among animals. They react to stimuli—or do not react. The functioning object is one that leads to further action and to the experiences consequent on such action. The object-in-use becomes a *source* of further differentiation. It controls what is found out about other objects. Indeed, the stone becomes an object, rather than a disorderly variety of qualities by the same status that it occupies as an extension of function. The rule is this: No functioning object, then no object at all. (Consider the difficulties of the psychological empiricists—Locke, Berkeley, Hume—in putting together a variety of qualities to make an object.) The *status* of object is an accompaniment of function. Every discovered object requires another functioning object as its authority. If marble is a soft stone, it is because it can be scored by a flint, as glass by a diamond. Length, weight, time, all depend on objects, which are not perceptual but functional. The wine-dark sea depends on grape juice. Consequently early speech is metaphorical. In a metaphor one object assumes the status of identifying another—as hard as a diamond, swift as an arrow. Emerson makes this point, and he was a poet with a feeling for the assimilation of words to acts.

What I do not think was the origin of language was a process of intellectual labeling. Nobody said, "I dub thee 'stone,' " as if he (1) "perceived" a stone and (2) had a supply of words, assigning one of them to that object. Given words, one can make others, "Kodak," for example. But the problem occurs because animals had no dictionaries, no prior supply of words like a box of labels.

There is another step: The functioning object needs a name if it is to be distinguished from a perceptual variety of qualities. It requires a *sign*. It is my stone, this stone, the stone, the stone-that-makes-arrowheads. All such expressions are functional and active. They are also illustrated in primitive speech. How this came about in particular I do not know. Nobody recorded the origin of language, the cry that made a stone peculiar, or made it yours or mine. I say only that the word summoned the stone, made it an object. This is magic. There was a notable lack of magic in the account of experience given by the psychological empiricists. They had no living word.

What I am unwilling to say is "There is the world, and here are the signs." That seems to me impossible, a very strong word. It is this consideration that keeps me from finding merit in an "explanation" of language, as if one already faced a state of affairs apprehended without words and then told how words emerged. I say they occur in functioning and that the alleged prior world—including animals—cannot be perceptually presented.

7

The Act as Unenvironed

It is notable that where act or utterance has been alleged, there has been some factor, or element, of infinity—some force, some order that fails of identification as a specific object. To "do" geometry is not to bring about a specific and terminating sequence of events or consequences of an event. It seems one cannot put an end to quantity or to space. One number, one space leads to another, as one word leads to another. One cannot answer the question, Why do you study mathematics? if an answer is to be given in terms of a terminating satisfaction, which having been attained, one turns to other objects or purposes where no mathematical factors are operative. I use a rip-saw but lay it aside when I need a hammer. But we meet arresting statements, such as "The world is mathematical" or that it is spatial, temporal, qualified. The limited itself leans on the unlimited. These are ancient manifestations of the locus of a doing that is without specific stimulus or terminating sequence. You can put a stop to malaria but not to numbers and suchlike infinities.

A further element or factor of the unlimited where action has been alleged is the person, mind, soul, spirit. As with the classical "categories," the mind is unlimited or allied with the unlimited. One cannot walk away from it. One does not claim to have a mind for any specific reason. One happens to have a cold and (with aspirin and whiskey) one hopes to be rid of it, but there is no way of getting rid of one's mind. This has often been noted. Faustus asks where Hell is located and receives a characteristic answer: "Why, this is Hell, nor am I out of it." And elsewhere, "Thou thyself art Heaven and Hell." It was the skeptic who had very early noted his identity with the ever-accompanying mind. The genuine skeptic is a rare bird and is no more manageable by another than by himself. But if he be the *author* of his universality then the autonomy that accounts for him must also save him or nothing else can do so.

It is the immediate and the universal that is unenvironed. Short of that no act can appear. Let what is considered an act appear as an environed event, and it will disappear into the circumstance in which it is allegedly found. There, its autonomy will be nullified.

There lingers a tendency to see an act as a "response." The response is specific and it is occasioned by the equally specific "stimulus." Furthermore, the object that is to be affected by the stimulus shares in specificity. Suppose one calls that recipient of stimulus a "stimulee." It changes under the influence of a stimulant, or at least in conjunction with a stimulant. The more specific the stimulee, the more determinate is also the stimulant. Neither is unenvironed.

In this way it then becomes impossible to discover an act. The dice are loaded. One would have to be very foolish to claim that in the conditions set for discovering a specific response of stimulee to a stimulant, one could come upon an act that is necessarily not conditioned. The premises do not allow it.

Because the stimulee is specific, it then becomes absurd to say "I am reacting to a stimulant" or "You are so reacting." The obvious catch is in the lack of specificity of the stimulee, the personal pronoun or the alleged person. The person does not appear as a specific object among other specific objects. Consequently no stimulant can be applied. The assumption that there are "persons" who react to specific stimulants has had a characteristic consequence. It is that the "response" is irrational and incalculable.

An indeterminate stimulee can give no clue to what the response may be. But a less obvious consequence ensues:

neither is it clear to what the indeterminate stimulee is responding. The stimulant becomes as indefinite as the stimulee. To what the nonspecific ego may be reacting has no prior specificity. The stimulant then becomes, as we say, "subjective." What I "do" is then stated as whatever the stimulant "means" to me. Such a stimulant entails no determinate response. What, then, can be said about the stimulant? It loses its specificity as the response, which it is to provoke, varies with an indeterminate stimulee. What becomes of a stone on the shore of Lake Superior when one stimulee ignores it or kicks it away and another stimulee picks it up and puts it in his pocket? The stimulant becomes as undefined as the stimulee.

So, if one demands specific stimulants, one requires an equally specific stimulee. The unenvironed stimulee leaves one wondering about the stimulant—*his* stimulant, since there is no other on the premises.

The aversion to the unenvironed stimulee entails a reluctance to abandon the specificity of the stimulant. We seem not only to saddle the act with a ghost but also to forsake the common world of determinate objects. That is a very serious matter. We might settle for the ghost as agent, but not for objects that vary in their meaning with every unspecified agent. What an object may be to another person we learn by what he does about it. Let that doing be itself unenvironed and nothing in the object commands or restrains. The primrose by the river's brim varies in its character with the act of the free agent. Butterfly weed takes its meaning from the mower who spared it in Frost's poem.

If seeing had no limitation, no one would be color blind, nor would sight and sound be different modes of quality. Infinity of the stimulee—unenvironed perceptions or actions—reduces every object to an equal indeterminancy.

Our hesitation over the free agent expresses this complementary reluctance to credit the indeterminate object. A free agent reveals no limited primrose. He confuses the environment, neither commanded nor restrained by it. The stimulant is lost because it lacks specific character for such an alleged stimulee. This is the other side of the free or unenvironed act. This is what we resist if only in a vague and troubled way. We cannot allow objects to "mean" no more and no other than they happen to mean to any number of unaccountable agents. If the agent is unaccountable, so is whatever the primrose may be to him. This is a consideration that haunts us but is not usually made articulate. It is usual to dismiss the free agent because he is indeterminate in the manner of objects; that the object is also threatened has complementary importance and force.

If we had our objects in the absence of all acts, the case against the act would be irrefutable. But it is said by many that we learn by doing. What is it that is thereby to be learned? Action, if unenvironed, as it must be, teaches us nothing about particular objects. To afford instruction the act must be already allied with particulars. We learn how to drive a nail by wielding a real hammer, how to hit a tennis ball by wielding a racket. Learning by doing is incorporate. It does not show us an aloof, disembodied, and ghostlike agent directing alien hands or other tools.

Learning by doing has long been recognized but has had a rival. It marks the craftsman but not the scholar, the sage, the saint. A "higher learning" has long been associated with a separation from particular doings and particular skill. The seven "liberal" arts were not defined as weaving, pottery, stone-cutting, archery, and such-like accomplishments. They include grammar, logic, arithmetic, and geometry. No learning of that sort carries information about particulars. It is rather associated with the ivory tower, with uselessness in the specific emergencies of hunger, sickness, or pleasures. The absent-minded professor has been a standard joke. Poor Thales, an astronomer and geometer, fell into a well and was rescued by a sensible servant.

Yet some sort of activity is required for the learning that is arithmetic and grammar. The arts and sciences demand effort and concentration. They are not acquired by the relaxed. They have the remarkable quality of bringing home to one some failure of control. They allow no evasion of liability for error or fallacy. If one is to claim command of one's doings, then one has also to avoid laying one's defects on a scapegoat. Such liberal learning has been called pure. We speak of pure science. If it is pure, it is because the act is also pure, that is to say, performed in the absence of limiting conditions. One learns how to drive nails or tennis balls apropos of peculiar objects and in the interest of peculiar results, whereas arithmetic employs no such specific objects in long division or in showing that there is, or is not, a last prime number. To the statement "We learn by doing" we would, then, require a supplement, "We learn by acting." This, however, is a statement that contemporary educators and learners find unwelcome.

It is not unusual to feel gratitude, or to find it in others, when a doing is corrected, but a person questioned on the control of his supposed action is likely to bristle. It is where a person feels some equation of himself and his acts that the suggestion of a lack of control evokes hostility. Psychologists dislike the suggestion that on their terms Pythagoras never had anything to say about triangles nor Aristotle about logic, that no individual Caesar crossed the Rubicon, that Ophelia was not mad but perhaps a bit odd. It does not appear from common encounters that persons are content with the learning acquired in specific doing. They say rather that they know arithmetic, logic, psychology, as well as "how to" drive nails or tennis balls. Many claim a knowledge of morals, values, beauty, political order, of wisdom and folly. If there is to be a learning that is other than that of our specific competences, it requires a nonspecific sort of control. We can hardly be said to have "learned" anything where no control whatsoever legislates true and false, achievement and failure. Learning occurs in a process. The word is a present active participle. We do not come upon "learning" as another object found on the beach or in a mine.

If we learn only by "doing," not by acting, then there may be no learning at all. Learning by doing has been captured by behaviorism, where stimulee and stimulant are both specific, with the result that learning events become "reactions" not actions, "responses" not responsibilities.

In the ancient world the skillful craftsman might be a

slave. The slave did not act. By law he had no will of his
own and had no personal rights or status. The very gods
came under suspicion in so far as they too knew how to
produce specific effects. They lost authority in the measure
that, among men, pure action supplanted specific doing. A
mathematically ordered world was a standing threat to the
alleged specific powers of the Olympians. A logical definition projected an order that was in conflict with the
merely occasional meddling of an angry or benevolent
deity. One may say that the gods were overthrown by
thought. But by what sort of thought? It was by a sort of
thinking that regarded itself as unenvironed. That was its
universality, and to that extent it differed from specific skill.
It was unenvironed because it declared the environment.
The slave and the Olympians had not done so. One should
not really be surprised if early scientists and poets considered themselves allied with controlling powers, as did
Empedocles and Horace. "The flight of the alone to the
Alone" does not differ in basic temper from the statement
that one lives in a mathematical world. It is a curiosity of
our time that those who patronize the old gods, calling them
"myth" and "unscientific," should so often be the same
people who allow no credit to the process that had de-
populated Olympus. That revolutionary result was not
achieved by the sort of learning that marks a specific skill.
It was achieved by adventures into the learning of action,
where a local control projected a universal order and so
invested the actual and present with the inherent power of
declaring the unenvironed. If one completes the sentence
"The world is . . . ," one has declared an activity, not a
perception, as immediate and controlling. Nor is the subject of that sentence a common noun qualified by attri-
butes, as if one had said "Sugar is sweet." It is in vain to
look about one for an act, an agent, or a world.

It is enough to make nonsense of the statement "The
world is . . ." if one admits to no learning but that of specific skill. And yet, men of all degrees have cherished their
sense of agency. This has usually taken a moral form. Supposed liberators have alleged that moral laws have been

imposed and that such imposition of rule had an ulterior motive. Yet the characteristic objections to rule have taken place in the interests of removing a blockage to personal agency. In dramatic cases, such as those of Socrates and St. Paul, the revolt from the imposed "law" expressed no vagrant egotism but rather discipline and fidelity. How could any law seem oppressive if it blocked no autonomy? Newton is not an oppressor of stars. Where there is no agent, the law is no tyrant. The testimony is general that the most acceptable rule not only permitted but proclaimed personal responsibility. We have demanded judgment in recognition of the act.

In our present historical position, we have stressed the overthrow of the gods but are unaware of the unenvironed action supporting that enormous revision. No advanced academic degree or journeyman's license qualifies for admission. Not to have acted is to be denied entrance to both Heaven and Hell.

We have demanded judgment as recognition of the act, and so also as evidence of the person. The person has been actual, not "real." Where judgment is not demanded, it appears as nonsense. It is as much nonsense to judge the nervous system as the solar system. We judge actualities, not realities. What has not been done or said leaves any judgment upon it a folly and, in the end, merely another phenomenon. Not to be judged is to be accorded no presence. On the other side, to judge is to present oneself, an agent, as a force, but as a force in alliance with the universal controls of action and not as a practitioner of a specific skill.

And so it has been said that "the man who has no music in his soul is fit for treasons, stratagems, and spoils." To have no ear for the music of the spheres—a mathematical harmony—is to lack order and direction and infinity.

8

The Environment as Actual

An act is unenvironed, yet it is necessary to have an "environment"—situation—if action is to be proposed or controlled. It has been environment that has then raised questions about the possibility of action and has sometimes denied action, engulfing it in circumstance. At the hands of theorists and philosophers, action has had rather the worst of it. The term "conditioning" has found rapid and general acceptance. It is more acceptable to say that slums make people than that people make slums.

The current evasion of action and of its consequences is not unreasonable if one considers that no one quite relishes being appropriated by circumstance. Perhaps one should say "expropriated" by circumstance.

So long as one considers any act as truly one's own, there is a good chance of meeting rebuke. One makes mistakes, and these remind the agent of his limits, a disagreeable result. In order to avoid rebuke, one would need to study the person, force, or region that administered it. Perhaps such forces could be placated or in some way controlled. But that requires application and trouble for oneself and schools for one's children.

The environment is the consequence of the functioning object. This environment is described in terms of actual operations, as a map of Massachusetts requires the instruments of survey. With respect to Massachusetts, one may say that Vermont is environment, like it or not.

The expression "the" environment is tricky. It suggests a single region that is everyone's environment. The definite article makes environment singular. Yet as a matter of history, there have been many environments, many accounts of nature and of man. Nor do we now say, after so many reconstructions, that the general plan has become fixed and final. I lived through part of the Darwinian revision. The Freudian discovery of conflict within the psychological has shown that environment is no seamless garment but rather generates confusion and arrest of action. The relation of space to time has modified earlier ideas of the simultaneous. I myself in venturing upon an essay in the examination of history, of dated-time as contrasted with clock-time, encountered reactions that showed I was disturbing an accepted and ahistoric view of the environment. In all such cases, it is remarkable that there is more than ordinary surprise or incredulity, as if oil had been found in the Adirondacks or a new beast reported in Africa or Australia. These radical revisions meet resistance or give rise to many books on the composition of a world. The environment—definite article—has always been unstable. It is this revision that is the same as history. Some people tell the truth, and how to be virtuous; historians tell how truth *was* told and virtue identified.

Is *the* environment then to vanish as another illusion? The curious quality of revisions is that they draw their appeal from conservative sources. If a man is to trust his own eyes, having also, perhaps, assisted vision with spectacles, then it is awkward for him to deny that when looking through a telescope he sees moons on Jupiter, upsetting as that observation may be for his view of the celestial environment. It seems that the egotism of man has emphasized novelty and has avoided crediting those *continuing* controls without which novelty is unintelligible, a miracle, a chaos. It has proved difficult to convince ourselves that we take a "look-see," an actual looking, and that moons on Jupiter or any other novelties derive their authority from the need of preserving vision. We preserve our functioning. What is the man saying when, as at Padua, he refuses to look through the telescope?

I feel strongly that functioning has been underplayed, or has been under suspicion in most accounts of man and of the environment. Revision is conservation of functioning. That is a premise of history. The empiricists have insisted on "findings" but have neglected to say why our findings could carry any conviction. It was to make findings authoritative that I urged the structural status of the "accident" years ago. At that time only one man, W. E. Hocking, saw the force of the accidental as constitutional. The empiricists resist any attempt to make their own claims authoritative. They have rejected a cognitive immediacy and properly so; but they have been blind to a functioning immediacy, to an actuality, which requires and absorbs data on functioning terms.

The basic objection to secularism, to science in its disclosures, and to history in its revisions, derives from a neglect of functioning as the immediacy of both self and of the environment. History is the record of the preservation of function, of an articulate immediacy. Even Descartes, mistrusting his senses, and unlike Hamlet finding no sensible and true avouch in his own eyes, fell back on mathematics, an *operation* of pure immediacy, not a datum but an orderly and productive doing, which commanded a world. Functioning is not a datum; it is the absolute occasion of data. Dogma is the discrediting of functioning. It proposes a world that is not the extension of the act. It is suspicious of the act and tries to control it, whether at Vatican or Kremlin or Jerusalem. Foolish people say that some dogma or other is "false" although they have no more readiness than the dogmatist to proclaim the authority of a controlling immediacy. The reason for the persistence of dogma is simply that the presented alternative has been no world at all and no environment. Consequently neither is there any ego who finds himself recognized in an environment. The "intellectual" has neither ego nor environment, not even to the point of arrest in action or thought.

Can one, then, use the expression "the environment"? Not if one means a datum, not if one proposes an object, not if one alleges a fixed and *a priori* state of affairs. Functioning maintains itself, and does so by proposing infinities, their controlled order, the relation of order to order, of psychology to logic, of physics to history, of clock-time to dated-time, and much else. The environment is the extension of an articulate and controlled immediacy never fully conscious of itself and of the modes of its maintenance. When, as in a democracy, the energies of men are basic to order, one has to expect great confusion in the resulting claims. And when these energies are taken to be desires rather than mathematics, logic, or history, one has lost a self-controlling immediacy. It is indeed notable that we have today an assault on institutions that are the functioning vehicles of enduring energies. So, the undergraduate, or even his professors, asks about the "relevance" of math or history, thereby advertising his lack of identity with the very powers, always the functioning objects, through which an environment is projected as the form of the immediate.

As far back as I can remember I was vaguely uneasy over claims about "the" environment. But I felt some attraction in stories, poems, geometry, logic—in what I would now say defined "the" environment. One does not "adjust" to environment as if it were come upon—external, a finding, an accident, the occasion of a specific and terminating response. The environment (singular) is met in the powers with which one is already in league—in having spoken, counted, or read a book by someone else who lived long ago. This singular environment is not conveyed through objects of perception but through the functioning objects, such as those named above. If one had a dog, one might name him "Zero," and he would learn to come at the call. But that would not make him a mathematician. Nor would I want him to be. For he might be concentrating on a quadratic equation and pay no attention. I want my dog to answer *specific* stimuli and not go wandering off into infinities. It is psychologists, not mathematicians, who train dogs.

I propose the environment, singular, as the extension or implication of functioning in a medium that is a functioning object of any sort. This environment has always been, and remains, an infinity, as the terms associated with it show, terms like almighty, omnipotent, all-seeing, omniscent, "the all-seeing, all-hearing, all-tasting, all-smelling One," the all-controlling, the alpha and omega, and many more. Yes, and one word leads to another, and there is no last natural number and no terminating cause for any specific event.

The high excitements of man occur apropos of the environment viewed as order and as infinity. There is a story, true I take it, that when Newton happened to hear a corrected figure for the radius of the earth—a figure that could establish the proposed "inverse-square" law as illustrated in the orbit of the moon—he reviewed calculations made years before using the new quantity for the radius. As he saw verification looming, he was overcome by such excitement and agitation that he could not proceed and then asked a friend to carry out the computation. The magnificent result was a universal law of motion, and he stood in awe of this powerful discovery. But this is a characteristic occasion of deep feeling. Another story, perhaps not true, tells that Thales, having solved a problem in geometry, went into the courtyard to make sacrifice to the gods. Great feeling occurs in the revelation of the ordered, infinite, and articulate environment, which is yet the extension of a controlled immediacy. There are many examples, for this vision is the locus of all exalted emotion. Milton, the Puritan, writes of "Il Penseroso," dissolving into ecstasy, with all heaven before his eyes, as he sat in the cathedral with its storied windows and there heard the pealing organ blow to the full voiced choir below "in service high and anthem clear." Keats was moved by Homer. Horace had erected a monument more enduring than bronze and would touch the stars with his exalted head could he be ranked with the lyric poets. But always there is in these excitements a sweeping composition, not a novelty of fact, and always it is the environment embodied in an utterance, in an equation, in the Parthenon or Amiens, in the Second Inaugural. There is here no termination response of the psychologists and pragmatists, but a potential, a projection that appears in the very voice that expresses and enacts it. The infinite and the finite are dialectical. The sense of the environment—definite article—occurs in the vehicle, which is finite, but not as a cognitive finitude, rather in the act; not in any object of perception but in the functioning object that is the embodiment of control and is both freedom and command.

If today "act" is a discredited and naughty word, it is because no composition of energies can appear in cognitive and empirical accounts of man and nature. The environment has been shattered into bits and pieces. I do not blame the physicists so much as the psychologists. Either they have no environment at all or else they borrow one from physics and mathematics. Neither physics nor mathematics is an "adjustment" to specific stimuli with terminating and pragmatic satisfactions of mysterious and arbitrary appetites. But under the influence of psychology, even those noble sciences have become mere tools and instrumentalities. The excitement of a Thales or a Newton then becomes a triviality no different from a burst of rage or a passing pleasure. I say out that the world is quite as much emotional as it is spatial or causal. Say the contrary and you reduce every arresting moment, every organizing action, and every person who manifests a world, to a triviality. Not even quite so little; for what composition may be, or utterance of any sort, or the person who speaks and acts, cannot so much as be found in discrete data. What is happening before our eyes is that adjusting to the environment has brought about the *abolition* of environment.

The other end of environment is the individual, and he has vanished with the environment. Where the world has no energy, neither has the person. It is a matter of record. Without persons, no environment, for it is the organization of their acts and utterances. That nature is more than a vague appearance is a consequence of some composition made by a person and illustrated in some activity—a word, a motion, a work of art, a mathematical proof. Suddenly one sees not *a* house, but *this* one, and the environment spreads from that and is composed, where before it was a stream of consciousness. One sees not a tree, but this one as it organizes a prospect because it stands in some personal connection. There, then, is the real world, and not a phenomenal one. There are also special environments. History studies their pretensions and their contributions to the environment.

Many have tried in vain to distill reality out of appearance. The philosopher's stone is supposed to transmute base metal into gold. It is not Everest that is "there," but a person, a man, a woman, even a child. That is the philosopher's stone. The actual is the watershed that permits the distinction of appearance and reality and generates both. In the end, authority is in the person who *reveals* an environment. Few do. But where there is grace and genuineness, one is under arrest. Persons stir no emotion except as they are revelations, and this is the immediacy of the actual, of functioning, and of its manifestations. Isaac Newton, the man overcome by the majesty of order, is not what we nowadays want. His laws, of course, are very handy when it comes to moving things around. Then they acquire "relevance."

A turn here: the individual (and so action and motive) is not discovered as an unconnected absolute. Motive and intent do not show in a present that owes nothing to its past. Why say this? Because it is often supposed that an event not in the order of anonymous nature could be only an abrupt and unordered event, an anarchic event. Action, then, has suggested a repudiation of order, at most an alleged interference with the order of nature and, in some cases, with the control and order of the supernatural. At worst, the alleged action and motive are nonsense, not even interference.

Science and action have in common that neither deals in abrupt catastrophe. Each presents a continuum. Motives and intentions get identified in a continuity of action. Why do I, or did I, go to the post office rather than to the grocery? To give an answer is to assume that some action *had been going on.* Otherwise the question has no basis—or "postulate" or "frame of reference." The answer is given in terms of what had been going on. In terms of the continuum of science, the statement "I go to the post office" (or Sammy does) makes no sense. Nobody ever thought it did. Science itself collapses where measuring, counting, reasoning, handling, looking, and so forth do not embody and have not embodied a continuum of action. If no verb, then no science and no scientist. And, if no past tense—as previous saying, doing, inquiring—then no science.

If one asks "What is the *motive* of the scientist?"—that is, what moves him, what allows one to identify him as agent—one answers that his energies are those inherent in the order of statements identifying nature. There is no nature to be known and described in an abstract present.

I find this difficult to say. Nature may be the "Not-Me" (Emerson), but this "Not-Me" is no present "datum," no magical apparition nor yet an absolutely alien region. Nature is a historical achievement.

I come back to the continuum of action mentioned above. No motive is found apart from some mode of the continuum of action with which one is identified. Action of any sort has a historical basis. On such a basis, one acts as scientist, lawyer, economist, craftsman. It is now time to stop looking for motives and intent in an alleged state of affairs not itself identified in the energies that define and have sustained it.

Energies flow from one's world, as any world projects the active self. In ancient times there was a negativist note, as in stoicism, and this because nature itself was not yet energetic and historical.

The universal is the form of the ACTUAL. Except as a person is a universalist, his supposed acts become atomistic, discrete, episodic, and not even his own. Do not look for the *person,* for his *acts* or his *motives,* in an alleged region not the projection of his doing. If you want a person's "motives," you will come to his general outlook, to his world. Short of that no motive can be assigned, and the supposed act fades into "reaction" or "response," although those terms are indefinable.

9

The "Presupposition" of Universals

While not grammatically at fault, the expression "the universal" may cause confusion if the noun is not recognized as requiring a plurality rather than a single entity. As a unity the universal has been self-defeating. "All is water" (air, fire, Brahma) assigns a name to the undifferentiated, to what has no *distinguishing* name, where even a name dispels the alleged unity, for then one has *both* the unity and also the name. Besides, a name generates a plurality; "unity" entails its opposite, "plurality"—another word.

This has been a problem lurking in all attempts to name "the universal" as a single entity. The "One" falls apart in being named. So the Vedandists reject "name and form"— the ultimate basis of all misology and of the mysticism of the inarticulate.

The unity without plurality does not unify. The plurality stands as illusion and has often been so indicted. The quest for integrity (integer, unity) then seeks to rid oneself of alliance with the many and *therefore* of the articulate. "Of making many books there is no end"—not only no terminus, but also no "end" as purpose or intention, as a present control that directs and organizes the utterance or the limitless content of appearance or of reality.

Confident pluralists repel any limit, must do so in order to retain their rejection of unity. They want no "block universe," no *ultimate control*. They equally repel any *local control* operating on the maintenance of order, which is a universal. They are neither finite nor infinite and can generate neither term. All rules are off. Rule limits; rule also projects an infinity. They will have neither.

So, if one is to require any universal that has a name, it will not be the undifferentiated unit. That has no name, not even the name "One" as against the "Many." Any articulate universal is not *the* universal. Space, time, cause, quantity, quality, and so forth, are universals, but also distinguishable. Multiplicity then occurs *in universals themselves*. Not only so, but short of such multiple universals no other multiplicity can be named or discovered, no multiplicity of particulars; no maple tree *here,* but an oak tree *there;* no leaf budding or falling *now* but not *then;* and for *this* cause or reason, *not* for some *other*. Any particular invokes its universal. Short of numbers one does not have ten fingers rather than twelve or none. Yet it has often been assumed that while particulars were known, universals were dubious. How one reached them, indeed, how the idea or sense of universals could be suggested, remained obscure. It was said that common properties of particulars could be observed, although nothing common was, or could be, an item of observation. The broad result was that no universal could be known, could occur as an item *within* knowledge.

If the universal is not "known," is it a "presupposition" of a *cognitive* sort? This is a very difficult matter. But it appears that any universal is necessarily not fully illustrated in any actual experience. The causal rule—or any other— guarantees a *lack* of actual order. This, I find, has been generally overlooked. One has to make some pretty radical statements in that connection. For example, that there are not "known" events that are *thereupon* examined for their causes. Uncaused events lack certification.

The "cause finder" should not, then, be imagined as finding causes for events known to him, but not yet equipped with causes. It appears that such precausal knowledge of events has been a view commonly taken.

Here is an event; what now is its cause? That seems common sense. Knowledge of causes is then made to seem as an *addition* to a prior acquaintance with objects, things, changes, events.

The universal rule of cause has been called *a priori*. It is overlooked that identified events, not yet causally explained, have an apriorist status; that is, *all* causes are to be looked for. To look for causes presumes the *prior* events. It is this prior status of *events* for which causes are now to be looked for that forces an apriorist status on the rule of *cause*. One is to enforce upon events an order they do not now have, an order not the same as the identification of an event. First the event, then the search for the cause, appears to be a common way of construing the state of affairs. *There* is the world; what is its cause? To raise questions of cause is then to have assumed the apriorist status of events. Events are prior to causal explanations.

This, I believe, is no claim peculiar to me. It was the position to which Kant addressed the first *Critique*. His argument was that nobody has, or perceives, or identifies an event apart from universals, including cause. In so saying Kant was repeating classical views. Knowledge comes in the formality of the "categories."

Nevertheless the conviction that we do "look" for causes is widespread. It must have some sort of plausibility. We give some credit to events when *not* knowing their cause. It is proper, then, to ask why we would look. Why not be satisfied with the event? Why impose upon it a rule, which—on the premises—it does not need to be perceived, known, recognized as an event? The causal rule then appears as a gratuitous imposition.

The criticism of the authority of the causal rule has been based on the claim that cause does not appear in the objects or perceptions that are *prior* to the causal question. The same claim has been made about *all* universals. We do not need them in order to perceive objects. The content of consciousness requires no universal. This goes back to the cynics. It reappears in Berkeley and Hume. In my day all universals have been called "pseudo-concepts." Why would there be a "problem" of universals if the universal were as immediate as perceptions, objects, events?

The rule "every event has a cause" is not so much false as it is nonsense—if one sees events as *prior* to the causal order, let those events be described in any way whatever. There lurks the feeling, or the conviction, that where there are universals we have *meddled* with a state of affairs that is prior to universal rule. We have *intruded*. And that feeling is supported by the premise of events about which the question of cause—or other universal—is subsequent. We try to impose the universal. It is not there originally. Hence it is not only cognitive nonsense, it is *arbitrary*. Who is any man that he should impose upon events an order not essential to the perception, recognition, or identification of events?

The picture, then, is that the notorious *prior* quality of universals is *posterior with respect to events*. We have the events; we then, and only then, look for causes, which, on the premises, are necessarily not present in the event itself or in *any* event.

But the rule of cause carries also the suggestion that we *ought* to ascribe cause and look for particular causes. It is not said that, of course, nobody need seriously concern himself with causes, that such occupation may be amusing or diverting or that it leads to many interesting arrangements of events if one plays that game. There is a feeling that cause-finding is more than a private peculiarity, a gratuitous connecting of one event with another. An uncaused event—or one without effect on other events—seems rather an illusion or a dream than a genuine event. How would one report an event that had no cause and no effect? For, of course, if every event has a cause, then every event *also* produces effects. If I say "It is raining," but you find no moisture on the grass, you are likely to charge me with imagining things. But why should you if events can be found without controlling antecedents or consequences?

It has been claimed that since every event has a cause, nature must have a *cause*—the "cosmological proof." But it has not been claimed that nature produces an *effect*. It has not been considered odd that there be a first cause, or that there be a final effect, although a final effect, that is, an object without effect, is no less absolute than a first cause. The moral of that is that the cause-effect order of events has seemed to require an *exemption* at both beginning and end. It is as if cause-effect took place apropos of some immediacy, some "reality" perhaps, some totality, some state of affairs that was *not* identified in terms of cause-effect. This persuasion has been quite as persistent as the rule of cause. But it has been overlooked as an assumption made where the causal rule is asserted or presumed. It appears that cause-effect comes to a *stop* somewhere, at the beginning and also at the end. So, one has an uncaused cause or an ineffective effect.

This exemption from the cause-effect rule reappears in the alleged event for which a cause is then to be found. Just as the first cause is not identified in terms of cause-effect (it being uncaused), so too is nature identified as without effect. The event, like God and nature, is not *identified* as constitutionally either caused or effective. How an event, so construed, would be caused, or how it would be effective, is as much a mystery as how the first cause produces effects, or how that first cause stands apart from any cause that produced it.

The "presupposition" of causal order conflicts with the *status* of an event allegedly not identified as both caused and effective. To say that the event *must* have a cause is to say that it is not *discovered as an event* until the cause—and the effect—are part of the discovered event. Why look for the cause of any event if the event can be asserted in the absence of all causal-effective order? If, on the other hand, the event is identified as initially both caused and effective, why invoke a "presupposition"? It needs none in that case.

Wherever I have found problems and difficulties over cause-effect, it has been because some event or reality has been asserted apart from a constitutional order of cause-effect. Consequently that order, if insisted upon, has to be imposed. This imposition is then resisted. You might as well impose cause on God as on an "event" not constitutionally causal, or demand that nature produce effects. The "presupposition" impeaches the status of some immediacy to which it is to be applied. Either that, or else it is super-fluous.

This, I take it, is the reason for the controversies over cause or any other universal. We cannot *apply* such rules to events or entities alleged to have been discovered without them. There is nothing to which such rules do, or can, apply that does not resist the application.

As presupposition, the causal rule is the denial of its own universality and necessity. It is not presupposed without *also* presupposing something else that is not causally iden-tified. Of this *other* presupposition, the causal rule gives no account.

It appears, too, that while the causal rule is treated as a presupposition, the event to which it applies has not usu-ally been treated as equally a presupposition. The quality of "presupposition" has been reserved for universals, for rules and order. It has not been attributed to events. But the event does not exhaust the state of affairs to which a presupposition is to be applied. Besides the event there is the *perceiver* of the event, or the *claim* that an event has occurred. This is the *third* member of the transaction. And it is solely by virtue of this third factor that the *status* of the event is secured. That status is acquired; it is attributed. The event is regarded as an assurance. Wood burns; we do not "know" the cause; but we perceive the burning. We perceive, too, that not all wood is burning. We say that *some* wood burns, some not. Nor is it the case that wood exhausts experience, that it is the *sole* object, that burning is the sole change. Wood is not stone. Stone does not burn; water does not burn. The statement "wood burns" is not an isolated absolute. If it were, why would one raise the question of a cause? And what is more, *who* is it who could then raise the question? The status of the event—wood burning—is the consequence of a presupposition, namely of the occurrence of wood and its burning in an experi-ence. The *assurance* of the event is not the event, it is the alleged *status* of the event. This assurance requires a presupposition. Apart from such assurance, the question of cause has no basis for having been asked.

This presupposition—that there are events, and that their status is derived from their presence to a perceiver—has also been attacked, and both soberly and warmly. We are to credit events in the *absence* of *all* presupposition. The event is to be an absolute. If so, it loses status as event. It has no setting. It is not *an* event. It exhausts the moment, and no moment is then *not* another moment. For "not" is a universal and a presupposition, an "organization word" not another discrete event, taking no account of any other.

The event has to be rescued as the price of proposing to place it in a causal order—or in any other order whatsoever. But that events are inherently organized is both a classic claim and one that has been resisted. The business of radical empiricism has been to resist the inherent order of any alleged event. But if such inherent order is denied, if the event stands without order, then we are not dealing with "presupposition" but with an arbitrary and mysterious imposition. On the premises, there is, then, a basis for resisting the rule of cause, or any other control.

Where such inherent order in the event has been denied, the perceiver, the forum in which the event appears, has also been denied. Where an alleged event has no periphery—wood *and* stone—neither has it a center.

Thus, that there are events, a claim underlying *both* the assertion *and* the rejection of causal rule, is a claim that cannot be sustained. The event is lost. It has no status. No question about it can be raised. It is immune to any and all questions. The absolute event amounts to this: "Ask no questions." Also, "Make no claims." Also, "Make no denials."

All that is rather old stuff. It is, however, useful for the understanding of where we are today. It has its practical side, especially in education and politics.

So, where do we go? What is the source of the universal order, of the events to which it applies, and of the perceiver or knower of both? As the story is usually told, they dangle, so much so that each is an intruder or a stranger to the others. Are *events* the source of universal cause; universal cause, the source of *any* event; either or both, the source of the center, which entertains a *plurality* of events and the *distinction* of event and cause?

Well, I will avoid exercising my patience over the strange neglect of the actual and sole locus of all these terms—that locus being utterance. It was a remarkable feature of my schooling that what was so, or not so, had no relation whatsoever to what anyone said. This separation of utterances and what was really so was not, of course, peculiar to *my* experience. It was a general assumption and had been made whenever a statement had a cognitive aim. Cognition aimed—if not at the unutterable, as with certain mystics—at a state of affairs with which any utterance about it had nothing to do. There was, of course, the famous "ontological proof," where at least some "ideas" or thoughts carried a warrant of a reality. But even then this warrant lay in the idea, not in the utterance. One "had" an idea. Where it came from was a mystery, but it was none of one's own doing. A cat could *look* at a king and a man could *speak* of a king without thereby prejudicing the question whether it was *really* a king that was perceived or was being talked about. If one said "The cat sees the king," one could be mistaken; perhaps it was not the king but a duke or bishop.

All this is the consequence of a cognitive aim. To equate either one's perceptions or one's words with what was really so was to lay oneself open to charges of illusion or dogma. Nothing that anyone said could, on the premises, go unchallenged. To slight the challenge was to prove oneself no longer concerned with the truth as expressed, or wanting to express itself, in some utterance. If anyone said "It is so because I say so," the reliability was transferred to the person of the speaker from the words spoken. The warrant is no longer in any properties of the saying—grammatical, logical, postulational, dialectical—but in the person of the speaker. The word of God was warranted because it was God's even though nobody could understand it. It passed understanding. To this day the words of Jesus draw their

authority from the authority of the speaker. That was not
the case with the scribes and Pharisees: it was not their
personal authority that warranted their words or enforced
their commandments. Even Plato's demiurge "looked to
the patterns," a remarkable consideration, very Athenian,
very intellectual. The cognitive temper hears no word
gladly; it hears critically because it hears only a word. No
word is ever its own warrant. How could it be when it is
"about" something else, and about something else that
stands apart from all words?

So, we put poets and mathematicians outside the tellers
of "truth" and mistrust the fascination they exercise upon
us. This is not because what they say is cognitively dubious;
it is because it is not cognitive at all and does not pretend
to be.

Suppose that it is admitted that there "are" words. It is
"known" that there are words. They have some sort of
reality, some sort of "real" existence. But if so, then, on
cognitive premises, the word and any utterance must occur
in a region that no word presents or declares. This is the
basis of "behavioral science." Utterance is "behavior," and
behavior is part of an alleged reality that no utterance
defines. No one then asks whether or not a statement is
"true." That question gives a status to utterance *vis-à-vis*
the real world, or, similarly, to ideas or thoughts, and to
the present person. To "know" that there are words is to
have shifted their status to a region not constituted by any
utterance. Words as "known" are not words as uttered.
The word known is not a word; the word uttered is not known.

No one can say what a language is "about." The question "What are you talking about?" is answered only where
the object of talk has been defined by talk. But the question
"What are you talking about?" can be neither asked nor
answered in general. To say what the talk is about is to
limit its content, and to do so in ways that are uttered.
Thus: "I am talking about the maple tree in my front yard,"
a sentence full of formalities and universals. But one cannot talk about God or the universe. Even the *name* of God
was not to be spoken, and there is a deep propriety in that

prohibition. The god who can be *named* becomes subject to the controls, or order, of utterance. The Greeks, but not the Jews, came to an ineffable finality that was not a god only but the totality of being. Its climax was the unmoved mover, or the One of Plotinus.

This sense, or feeling, or result, that no totality can be talked about is the controlling source of all mysticisms. That totality is the sole immediacy. Nothing talked about is immediate. It is mediated. The mediated—*without immediacy*—is an illusion. The immediate without the mediated loses "name and form" and all articulate content. The mediated, as much as the immediate, is nothing to be talked about as if talk and deeds had nothing to do with its status.

I accept the nominalist claim that universals are only voice—*vox, praeterea nihil*. But the nominalist, dealing in nouns not in verbs, then concluded that since a universal was only a voice, it was unreal. What he did not recognize was that "real" was *also* a universal and a voice, that is, was the immediacy of utterance and of action. The negative is a voice and only a voice. In pure being, whether physical or psychic, there is no negative. The negative is the assertion of an absolute immediacy and it is the actuality of the person and of his finite presence. It is his ultimate risk. But it is an actuality. It is the ontological assertion of presence and of the world that ensues. It is a word, an utterance, an act. This immediacy is not talked "about," as if negation was to be found, if at all, in a region not constituted by voice and action. Negation is a universal, *"Omnis determinatio est negatio."* Whereupon Spinoza conjured up a substance without determination and negation! Hegel came closer to the articulate: "Substance is subject." It is the doer and speaker, the maker of a historical career. Yet even Hegel discounted the actual and the finite. It was this that made him eligible for adoption by the Marxists. They resist the actual, the finite, the personal and individual. They are suspicious of utterance and want it to conform with a reality not constitutional with the word. It was this supervision of the here-and-now that, in Hegel, made the historical process subordinate to the Idea. The Marxists embraced the subordination but rejected the Idea for Matter. Hence, "dialectical materialism." They want history, but no authoritative present. They want a universal that is not a word, not an action, not the actuality of presence.

Our education has become nonsense when no word is commanding because it is spoken and then maintains itself in its own medium. Christianity accepted the authority of the word, but not of the world generated by utterance. "In the beginning was the Word," a tremendous assertion, but the word at any beginning is not the word at the end—if, indeed, it was a word that was at the beginning. But what has been the result? In rejecting the eternal word, we have rejected all words in favor of behavioral science, where no word declares the real. The word, then, is neither the temporal nor the eternal. It is a non-entity in terms of an unspoken reality.

We have not won the temporal by rejecting the eternal. We have lost both. "What is the relevance of history?" is a question I have been asked. What is the relevance of any present, of any here-and-now, of time itself, becomes the practical force of that question. One cannot now speak for oneself as present. Our freedom of speech and of the press has come to mean that no word is authoritative. The authoritative word is taken to be the destroyer of freedom. It is regarded as dogma, prejudice, apriorism, egotism, and much else associated with any utterance that takes us captive.

The word that does not declare the world has no authority. Action is no intellectual presupposition. It is the source of universals. They are its form. No action, then no form. The record on that is clear. Form and content combine in the act. Without agency, no specific cause. Purpose and cause are both immediacies or else both vanish. But this immediacy is that of the act. To find out causes is only to sustain purposes.

The act is the self-declarative. This declaration is an utterance, as when one counts. This utterance is a universal, in this case quantity. It is there that the person has made his appearance. It is there that a world has made its appearance as an order and as an infinity. The act, the person, the here-and-now, the word, the world, appear together. If Plato required a credit in geometry for admission to the Academy, it was as much to secure the attendance of a person as to assume a basis for projecting a world. Points, lines, planes are utterances. They are not things. They are not ideas. So treated they gave rise to insoluble problems. The tortoise never got from *a* to *b*. There was no *a* or *b* to start from. That was the consequence of treating motion as cognitive. Space, time, quantity, change, are indeed not cognitive. They are all actual. They are not real; they are not imaginary.

Cause is not a presupposition imposed on events lacking a causal order. Any identified event is a consequence of an active control, if only of "looking," where some limitation of appearance is constitutional to the looking. Looking is a verb. To look is to be acting, to have identified objects by prior action and because of such action. The question "Does a stone burn?" makes no sense where nothing has been set afire.

Where there's a road there has been going. The wilderness is then less bewildering. Where there is a way, a procedure, a control, there has been a traveler. No way, no road, has manifestation as absolute prospect. The road is the course taken to have arrived. Without direction there is no going, neither departure nor arrival. A road is retrospective. It is the continuance of a doing. Passivity has no roads. It neither departs nor arrives. Where there is no path, neither is there a wilderness, the unexplored. Any path, any way or road entails not only the verb, but also the past tense of the verb. "Farther on" presumes the direction that had been taken. Until there has been a doing, there is no present doing. The continuum of action is the same as the action.

10

The Form of the Actual

We no longer live in a natural environment, but in an artificial one. Even nature itself has become artificial. It has ceased to be capable of description by eyes and ears, and is now understood in terms of yardsticks, clocks, balances, voltmeters, and an elaborate mathematical apparatus. "Back to nature" has come to mean back to ignorance. The functioning object does not alienate from nature but rather reveals it. Without the concepts and the instruments of science, we are not so much in the presence of nature as lost in the mist of vague subjective feelings and of the beliefs that grow out of them. These beliefs we call superstitions. It is not too much to say that a superstitious view of nature may be defined as any version of objects that does not stem from such artifacts as the instruments and concepts of physics.

We define nature through our acts, but not through such acts as occur in animals. Nature for man is the organized view of those acts that occur as measurement, or through observation with the aid of instruments. A yardstick is not a piece of pine or maple, it is a means of doing something. Its sensory properties are not what make it a unit of measurement. In the end, a yardstick is only what we say it is. The bar of platinum preserved in the Bureau of Standards has no "natural" length. It is not a yard long. But any other object, equal in length to that bar, is declared to be a yard long. This implies an active comparison. Objective length is a function of an act, and of a functioning object; it is never a fact, not even a "raw" fact or a "hard" fact.

Animals do not define nature, they are part of nature. They are part of an objective region that is suggested only when action has become artificial. In terms of sense and instinct the idea of nature as object does not occur, nor, of course, does the idea of person as subject. Sense and instinct do not put us in charge of any object, or of ourselves, for the best of all possible reasons, namely, that they convey no suggestion of either nature as object, or self as subject. This is one of the oldest of insights. The natural man has always been identified as the passive man, as the victim of his senses and of his appetites. He is only what he happens to be, and he does not know even that until by a *tour de force,* perhaps ascribed to revelation, he equates his true self with command, with thought or criticism.

Human nature has, from the earliest times, been identified with this active capacity. Sometimes this has been called "reason," or the life in accordance with reason. All such expressions indicate a need for control, for something more than passivity. But one should by all means take note that the active control of nature has frequently, and characteristically, absorbed the passive into the active, described nature in terms of Platonic ideas or Aristotelian categories or Kantian forms of judgment. On the moral side, an analogous appropriation of passivity to activity has occurred. Plato describes the love found in appetite as a preliminary form of disinterested love. The passions of men have usually, though not always, been viewed as essays at the good. In this way the parental, sexual, or pugnacious tendencies have acquired status within the controlled and self-directed life. Indeed, their very identification as passions is impossible save from the point of view of that control which finds them disturbing. Nature, whether as object or as feeling gets described in terms of order and control. Nobody finds nature in his senses or appetites; everybody discovers it as the integration and composition of sense and passion into meaning.

Nature is the order of our acts. It is pure action, for the

same reason that we call mathematics and physics pure science. Measurement and observation with instruments are pure acts. For that reason they are sometimes viewed as impractical. But counting, measuring, and observing with instruments set the stage for all orderly particular acts. They are generalized action. The mathematician may have no more information than an office clerk, but he knows how to get that sort of information. The physicist may be no more skillful than a plumber when it comes to installing water pipes, but he understands the general laws of liquids. When we want to learn about the difference between the dull meaninglessness of our sensory consciousness and the ordered region that we call nature, we go to the natural scientists. We encounter a lot of instruments and the theory of their use. Such a study is the price of establishing the region of nature. At every point that region has become artificial. No instrument in a laboratory is what it seems to be. It is not a sensory object, but a theoretical artifact with a meaning that only years of study can disclose. One might take great satisfaction in getting a clear idea of what it is to tell time, of how one sets up the conditions for alleging that two clocks are synchronous, for example, and of the general conditions that permit one to assert that two events are simultaneous, or that one event precedes another, and from what point of view. But one needs clocks and yardsticks, and these are functioning objects, and upon them rests the idea of that objective region called nature. When, today, we speak of nature, we no longer refer to sights and sounds, or even to useful objects controlled by rule of thumb for the satisfaction of some instinctual need. We mean rather a grand vision of order, and of an order that absolutely rests on the artifact and its theoretical meaning.

We live in this artificial environment. To speak of the natural or the social environment has become a commonplace of psychology. But such talk is less than accurate or rigorous. There is no natural environment, nor any social environment either, apart from the artifact, the instrument, the functioning object, and the symbol.

A science appears when the controls of questions have

been made explicit. Any question assumes a control. The answer is given in terms of a control. Years ago students in Physics 1–2 were started off with the question, How long is this copper bar? They made measurements. They did not engage in "Transcendental Meditation," for example. With respect to the science called physics, it is the measuring and calculating that are the universals. The universe of discourse of physics includes *procedures* of that general sort. To ask a question in physics—and by extension in chemistry, astronomy, geology—is to require an answer in the same terms.

Disputes have occurred over the proper way of asking questions. May one ask "why" Caesar crossed the Rubicon? It is not a question in physics. It is "unscientific" to ask "why." One is to ask only "how," and this in terms of the controls that define physics. Nor, of course, may one ask "why" one's questions are to be framed in just those controls and in no others. There was a time, not so long ago, when questions and answers in terms of the controls of physics were regarded as improper. At Padua the professors refused to look through Galileo's telescope. Currently the question "why" is not regarded as dangerous but simply as stupid. The universe of discourse that includes "why" has become a myth.

Further, the order suggested by the term "cause" is also in disrepute. There is no cause operating in a sum of numbers, in the properties of even, odd, and prime numbers, or in the relation of radius to circumference. Nothing "happens" to bring about such results, as if they might or might not occur. Nor may one ask what brings it about that clocks at opposite sides of a room are said to be simultaneous. Such simultaneity *defines* Euclidean space, but not non-Euclidean space. But, in contrast, how does malaria happen? Is it the night air, not the air of day, the diet, a mosquito, and which mosquito?

Math and physics are accounts of "The Nature of Things," *De Rerum Natura,* an old book title in both Greek and Latin. They do not account for Caesar's crossing the Rubicon, or for malaria and the absence of malaria last July, or for my having gone to the post office yesterday morning. The control suggested by "cause" has become "unscientific."

Mathematicians recognize that their knowledge does not express contingencies and that their statements are not "verified" or demonstrated by observation and experiment, as if a reasonable person needed to consider the possibility of alternatives. Mathematics and physics develop within their own orbits. Whatever seems to be happened upon in those steadily powerful modes of discourse has grown from their own requirements. They are not pensioners of circumstance; rather, they declare the universal form of all circumstance. They haunt whatever we may say in particular.

I insert here a reason for the disrepute of cause. It is that cause appears *in alliance with purpose and action,* with producing and preventing an effect. Passivity loses causality. The radical empiricists made that plain. Cause became a pseudo-concept. Among the accidents there were no necessary connections. This was, and remains, a powerful claim. It was an old claim. It was well recognized. In *The Paradox of Cause* I laid out the mutuality of cause and purpose, that is, of cause and local control. In so far as purpose, action, and local control are no part of the nature of things neither is cause. That is the paradox: on one side, cause appears as a universal; on the other side, any cause accounts only for the particular. Whatever is alleged to explain *all* events explains no particular event. It makes no difference whether the all-explainer be God or nature. In physics all change is absorbed into invariance, into the uniform and universal; in theology, into the inscrutable.

You can prevent damage to a crankshaft by lubrication and rid yourself of malaria by draining swamps and puddles, but nothing done can prevent the ratio of radius to circumference. As Carlyle remarked about Margaret Fuller, who accepted the universe, "By God, she'd better."

The famous argument to a first cause was not proposed by radical empiricists, who, of course, found no connections whatsoever between events and could put no restraint on anything whatsoever from happening. Cause was proposed by those who imagined that one event did entail a sequel, a consequence, a particular consequence. "Happy is he who is able to discern the causes of events," so Vergil. But such causes were regarded as properties of *objects*. We had no hand in determining any cause. The causal world was itself the grand object. But that this majestic object was "there" at all rather than "not there," or "there" in some other arrangement, required to be accounted for. To regard nature as an object, and to suppose further that any condition of any object is to be accounted for, is to require a cause of that object. *This* world, like *this* case of malaria, called for a determinant, quite reasonably on the premises.

When in 1781 Kant supported the claim, ancient and contemporary, that causal order (or any other sort) was no content of consciousness, not an appearance, he was not abandoning all structures to an abrupt and incoherent discreteness. His structured order did not, however, present an object or allow a totality of events. His structured order yielded no objective totality and *for that reason* disqualified an attribution of cause to nature. This upset the theologians and the famous cosmological proof. But, on the other side, it also roused the vocal hostility of radical empiricists, who allowed *no* structure to be inherent in their passive data of perception. But all that Kant had done was to put nature in the same status as its particulars, namely, phenomenal. Nature was not the "real," and this because it was no total object, but an organization *without limit*. Well, no infinite object has ever been a cognitive object. God has eluded cognition. Neither infinity nor the finite appears in atomized discreteness. Any alleged datum is absolute and miraculous and so generates *neither* infinity nor finitude. Both fall back on organization and on a continuum.

Like all others Kant had to account in some way for the alleged universal. He said it was *a priori*. We had no hand in discovering it. Where I allow myself to modify that great man is in saying, as I have been saying, that *we do have a hand in it*—the hand that picks up a yardstick, the tongue that tells time by the clock, the act that keeps a tally by cutting notches in a stick or making a notation on paper, where alone the expression $7 + 5 = 12$ or $a + b = c$ becomes manifest. I have been saying—*and it is a saying*—that the universal is the form of the actual, generated, enlarged, conflicting as the act maintains itself in a local control.

Local control appears in the functioning object. These include yardsticks, clocks, numbers, utterances of many sorts, and especially what is called "the body" as the center of functioning. Intellectualism nowhere shows its abstraction more plainly than in its attempt to treat the body as *a* body, another object or even as content of consciousness, in which nothing so gross as any body appears. On this point, it has pretty thoroughly abandoned common sense.

A person closely associated with his own body is not likely to reduce himself to a stream of consciousness, that unordered and passive variety, that essential helplessness, where the most elementary questions such as "Where am I?" or "What time is it?" or "How much are seven plus five?" or "Why do you go to the post office?" become impossible. One of the standing difficulties of universals— the pervasive difficulty—occurs in their not fitting into the psychological story of perception. One does not "perceive" what is pervasive, not present *here,* absent *there.* The universal is never *absent;* for that reason it is also never *present in distinction* from something else. *This* is a maple tree, but *that* is an oak. But numbers, for example, are not found or kept in one place but not in another, or units in the top left drawer and all the twos in the bottom right drawer.

Plato spotted the problem: what was the status of those words or ideas that "run in and out of every word we utter"? You can't "happen upon" any universal, as by going to Australia you happen upon an oviparous mammal, but not here in Berkshire County.

As items of knowledge, as *within* knowledge, universals have always been mysterious. I am saying that they are not cognitive at all, that they inform the act, as in going to the post office we become aware of what we are doing. As in saying "it takes longer," a longer time, to get to the fire house than to the post office, provided that one lives on

Elm Street. That is where I live. Then I am called narrow-minded. Surely I ought to be bigger than that, not so provincial, a citizen of the world, but not of Williamstown. What world is that?

One can see why, in desperation, universals have been proposed as "innate ideas," ideas, but innate, or in Plato's case as "reminiscence." I am saying that they are not "ideas" but actualities, and requiring the utterance that is their embodiment.

Sorry, but I feel that I have solved the "problem of universals." On cognitive premises they are indeed a problem. Nobody "perceives" a yardstick, clock, negative, the individual. Universals are discovered—forced upon us—in history, not in knowledge. Short of action and its partial organization, there is no history. Make no claim to the here-and-now as authoritative, self-defining, and world-projecting, and dated-time has no manifestation. Count your fingers and you launch the career of mathematics. Without the word there are no consequences. The midworld is the vehicle of all order and of the revision of order. It is the self-revisory.

Notice that the lack of connection, that is, of syntax, has been based on a view of knowledge not on action, on data, which are passive, not on facts, which are enacted.

All *consequence* is in the act. Scientific data occur as consequences of control, consequences of yardsticks, clocks, numbers, of measuring, of the verb.

I cannot get a hold on a person *except* as I take him at his word. But does he speak? Has he spoken? Can *he* appear in utterance? If his voice is not his own, why should he—or could he—listen to mine? If his voice is not legislative, why would mine be? A man must hear his own voice before he can credit another's. If he speaks, in what way, then, is he, the individual, present in his word? What sort of word would that be?

11

The Actuality of Ignorance

I have been suggesting that a universal is verbal, a verbal noun (counting, measuring). Cause has been lost where there is no causing, no doing. I would say, then, that no cause is ever "found." It is not that some causes are found and some not; none is found, if "to find" has only a cognitive force, not an active and purposive force. If no purposes (production and prevention), then no causes.

If cause is universal for orderly cognition of events, so is purpose.

In physics there are equations of orderly relation, but no causes. $S = \frac{1}{2}gt^2$ explains no event in particular. The order of nature is not determined by purposive acts. But it is wholly dependent on action, on purely formal action, on pure action. It is the formal order of any act concerned with any object. Thus $\frac{1}{2}$ is a quantity, but not the quantity of dollars in my pocket. But $\frac{1}{2}$ is discovered in an operation or, as I would say, in an utterance. So with all general properties of nature, with the S in that equation, with space, measuring, a yardstick, a functioning object. This is the midworld. This is not found. Nor is it a cognitive presupposition. It is the actual. Nature is not "what I may do" (Emerson); it is the form and projection of actual doing. Where there has been no doing, there is no universal and no nature. (To be outrageous: Einstein is wrong; nature ensues upon a prior doing, upon a past. The "square" in $E = MC^2$ requires that one shall have been counting and so has generated the relation of an exponent.) Remove the act and the "presupposition" remains a mystery, not a possibility, but a blank, a "pseudo-concept."

The locus of all universals is the midworld.

We speak of *all* events, or *every* event, and say that every event has a cause. We say, then, that cause is a universal, and then we raise doubts about cause in that status. But to speak of all events, or every event, is already to have universalized. All the "things"—words fail me—that are events have a common property. What is an "event"? Can one answer apart from some organization? Events in the plural have *some* connection. What is it? "Well," one says, "they are all in space and time." But this begs the question of universals. Or, "The event is what I perceive." Am *I* then the universal, as with Kant's "The 'I think' accompanies all perception"? The "I" as universal has fared badly. And it is a fact that where universals of nature are made dubious or rejected, so has the person disappeared. There is no "class" of "all events," like "all trespassers" where there might not be any particular trespasser. "Event" is itself a universal. It is not a cognitive term. It is not a logical term. It is an actuality. It is not psychological. It is not a sensory quality or a fortuitous and miraculous conglomerate of discrete "data." It falls into no prior frame of reference.

The corollaries drop out. For example, the scholar never deals with "real" objects; he deals with functioning objects—words, atoms, yardsticks, clocks, numbers, and so forth. Yesterday I mowed grass; does that make me a scholar? It is quite true that in that "real" world one has no logic, as James and B. F. Skinner declare. Logic requires utterances. Only the world as uttered shows a logical form—or a spatial and temporal form, or any other universal.

Well, it is risky and perhaps obscure to be affirmative. On the other hand, the affirmation shows the basis of any remarks one might make about events, cause, presupposition, purpose. So, I keep reverting to my controlling affirmations. No basic affirmation is cognitive. No basic affirmation alleges a "reality." There is no basic "reality."

What is basic is functioning. The evidence of functioning is not some reality, something "known." The evidence is the functioning object.

So, the statement "every event has a cause" names no real object. Every word in that sentence is either a universal or a verb, and the universals are all forms of a doing. Where would one "find" the objective equivalence of "every"? As object there is no "every." Yet the suggestion of universal cause is made dubious because cause is a universal and so goes beyond all cognitive verification. Unless we can speak of "every" event, we cannot propose a universal cause. So, we have employed a universal to raise a problem about a mode of universality. Discrete events suggest no "every." Each stands alone. One could not even say that one had many events without letting oneself in for various universals, for a center and an order that are not events and not cognitive. No question about the reality of universals is possible without begging the question. Where no universal is original, none can be suggested as a way of regulating the discrete. The "presupposition" is not applied to prior events lacking in universality. And one may note that the presupposition is not being presented as cognitive. Nobody "knows" that cause is a universal. Somewhere the not-known is involved to make knowing possible. What, then, is the source of what we do not know, without which we lose knowing?

I submit, on broad lines, that the world as "known" has never been plausible. There has always been some force, or being, not known, that gives assurance to knowing. This not-known basis of cognitive assurance has been sought as something known, as a reality of some sort. That has always failed. Knowledge requires an assurance, and this assurance is necessarily not known.

Well, I am suggesting what is not known. The act is not a cognitive mystery; it is not cognitive at all.

It is common to hear that in terms of whatever is alleged to be "known" the act is not discoverable. Whether that known object be nature or God, the act falls under suspicion. That is the root of the persistent problem of "free will," whether in B. F. Skinner or in J. Edwards. Knowledge must itself be dissociated from action. The known disqualifies the knowing. Tell what you "know" and you meet a demand for a warrant, and that cannot be supplied by alleging something known as warrant.

Philosophers have always invoked what was not known. Men of knowledge scoff at such proposals. They prefer the bankruptcy of knowledge to any authorization of knowing in terms of what is not known.

I am saying that this authorization is the act. It is author, it is the original. Where there is no author, there is no authority. I come back to verbs and to the actual vehicles of verbs, to the functioning object, to the midworld as the vehicle and evidence of both the objective world and of the individual.

"Higher learning" deals in functioning objects, not in "real" objects. The "drive" to learn more about numbers resides in numbers already articulated. It is one "word" that leads to another. An utterance, like Aristotle's "entelechy," seeks its inherently enforced transformation. That is the activity and work of the scholar.

Functioning is its own guide and its own energy.

Any utterance assumes control of further utterance. One proceeds to talk mathematics, physics, poetry. The form is both discipline and energy. One discovers the way to poetic utterance simply by uttering the poetic word. The sayings of the poet are controlled by the form or manner of his speech. Rhyme, alliteration, meter, precision are evolutions of that mode of utterance, quite as mathematics or physics ensue upon their peculiar controls.

It is true that when any utterance evolves on its own terms, the speaker has the odd sense of not speaking for himself. He is "inspired." The Muses direct him. He may invoke them, and has. But the mathematician and scientist is like the poet in not speaking for himself. It is no arrogant egotist who says that there is or is not a last prime number. The numbers speak, not he. He speaks in their name. Early pronouncements about nature impressed both audience and speaker as semi-divine. Lucretius and many of his predecessors spoke in a poetic form. When natural science spoke in its own form, it ceased to be presented in poetic form. For all that it continued to speak in a strictly formal way. The form imposed the content. Centimeters, grams, seconds, molecules, atoms, are ways of speaking. A yardstick is no more "real" than a rhyme. Neither is "real" as separable from functioning.

The actual is both form and content. All particular content derives its persuasiveness from its continuation of the actual. The yardstick and the room it measures are continuous; the maple tree and the word for it. The "real" is the content generated by the actual. The unreal is the confusion of functioning, something which, if seeing, I do not see; if measuring, correcting, saying, I do not come upon. It was an ancient insight that "non-being" was a lack, a deprivation, not another sort of reality.

But why bother about the real at all? Discredited metaphysicians talk about the "real," and nobody takes them seriously. When the "real" is spoken of as having a cognitive status, it becomes a bore to persons who pretend to knowledge. The distinction of "real *vs.* unreal" does not fall within any cognitive order. I wonder how it was possible to spend so much time in essays of discovery of reality when its opposite—unreality—fell within no mode of knowing. Do the operations of mathematics, physics, and logic come upon an unreality? And if they do not, what basis would there then be for claiming that they led to realities? In fact, it has come to be accepted that in so far as knowing employs any procedure or control it is embarrassed by the further question whether or not it has revealed a reality. Does any logically derived conclusion, because it is a logical conclusion, pretend to stand also as a reality? In fact, logic has been repudiated by some seekers for reality. But the same result haunts any method by which reality is allegedly found. Is seeing the same as believing? Not if "seeing" means only that the real is green or blue or grey.

The statement "The real is known" has never been plausible. Similarly, and by consequence, the statement "The real is unknown" becomes cognitive nonsense because nobody can say what it is that is unknown, namely, the real. As Royce once asked, "What is it that ain't?" And so, it has come about that talk of the real and unreal has been more and more avoided. Knowledge and "reality-unreality" are mutually exclusive. Knowledge has always reached beyond itself, or else fallen back on something prior to itself. Such eventualities or priorities are not discoverable in terms of the content of the controls of knowing. The statement "The maple tree is forty feet high" rates as knowledge; but the statement "I see a maple tree forty feet high" is vigorously challenged or patronizingly dismissed as nothing known or knowable.

I have been proposing that we accept the exclusion of knowledge and reality–unreality. Reality and knowledge do not suit each other and never have. Today people know a lot; the more they know, the more reluctant they are to entertain talk about reality-unreality. It is the ignorant who still find that distinction important. They go to church or embrace "dialectical materialism" and so become suspicious of men of knowledge as against men of faith or conviction. We regard the charge of "anti-intellectualism" as sufficiently damning.

Yet the men of knowledge are not quite nonchalant. They say it is a good thing to know, not to be ignorant. Ignorance is not bliss. It does not follow, of course, that if ignorance is not bliss, knowledge is any better. Perhaps neither is bliss. Yet we are urged to learn, to know, as if to know did put us in touch with something that gave status to knowing.

Where I cannot account for my ignorance, neither can I account for my knowledge. But in terms of my knowledge, I cannot account for the admission, or the claim, of my ignorance.

To revert to the beginning: the scholar deals in the actual, that is, in the controlling utterances, not with things known about. His business is with the midworld, with numbers, yardsticks, monuments. Whatever anyone calls "real" is a consequence of his actuality, or a local control, of which the universal is the form. On that basis he can also say that he is ignorant of much. After all, isn't it a bit comical to find this interest in "research" where no one can say—in terms of knowledge—that he is ignorant? Instead of having a "theory" of knowledge, I propose the actuality of ignorance. And that is no "theory" and cannot be. How do you "explain" knowledge was the question; how do you account for the claim of ignorance is my question. And if one is to answer it, one had better settle down to the actual. How is one to avoid dogmatic absolutism if one claims ignorance? Is it any less absolute than claiming knowledge?

12

The Constitutionally Incomplete

I recall a seminar when a colleague asked me to define certain words so that my sentences could be understood. The definition was to precede the use. It appeared that anyone who spoke should first define his words. This seems a not unreasonable requirement. We do, in fact, ask what a speaker means by a word, by "meson," "parameter," "Eurodollar."

The requirement appears less reasonable if made generally for all words. One would then be claiming that any and all words were to be defined prior to their having been spoken. The requirement that one define any word prior to its use in discourse would force one into a regressus in so far as the definition was also verbal. Problems of any continuum are ancient in their discovery and have been puzzling ever since Achilles, the swift runner, was declared incapable of overtaking the plodding tortoise.

In general, any continuum has failed to appear in the content of consciousness. For that reason syntax of any sort has fallen under suspicion. It is not empirical. Syntax is form, and form is procedure, and procedure is actuality. Achilles could not proceed. Nor, by the same token, had he ever reached the start of the race, having been summoned to the contest by the referee. The suspicion attending any momentum or continuum has persisted and is

widespread. The invariant has been a staple of the identifying thought, of knowledge itself, and of ethics also. I
have heard people speak of the "eternal verities." What does
not change in the midst of change?

People say, "Proceed in this way." They set rules. Then
we are brought face to face with some invariance. Many
rebel. They charge dogma, arbitrariness, authoritarianism,
prejudice. The liberal then retreats and apologizes for his
rules by calling them "hypotheses" or "postulates." So we
play at "Let's suppose." We play games. We may even
play at mathematics or logic. Or we may not.

Any continuum appears as the momentum of an immediacy. The momentous immediacy is the act. Only act has
consequences. The continuum appears as the universal, and
the universal only as continuum. Except as procedure, a
going on, a prolongation, no universal has been discovered
and all have become dubious or disreputable. As nouns all
universals have been rejected as making no appearance to
the sensuous and mortal eye. They have been seen, if at all,
only in the "mind's eye."

What I have been saying amounts to a relocation of the
universal not as the form of *content,* but as *the form of the
actual.* I put it in the verb, not in the noun, and not as a
noun. The continuum is in the verb. A geometric line is
"produced" and is cognitively elusive. Nothing seen is a
line, let alone a point. I am saying that there is no *cognitive*
postulate such as point, line, equal, and *not* equal. I am
saying that all such terms are procedural and that the continuum inheres in that procedure and nowhere else. I say I
live on Elm Street and go to the post office and count my
fingers and tell time and that it is in such actualities, and
there alone, that any continuum is suggested. So, I have
been saying that infinity is the form of finitude. If no verb,
then no universal such as space, time, and quantity. Similar
considerations apply to cause; do nothing and no cause, no
necessary connection, appears in the content of consciousness, in the data of passivity, a famous argument, not of
empiricism (which is a procedure) but of radical empiricism, which is without procedure and so is confined to

miraculous data that are never looked for because "look-ing" is a verb and an actuality. It is a here-and-now and it is a momentum, not a stasis. In terms of passive data, no basis for distinguishing seeing from hearing is possible. There is no syntax on passive terms. Syntax is actuality. It is not cognitive. It controls any alleged cognition.

Control has become a term of reproach. It has been fascinating to observe the complete helplessness of anyone supposed to exercise control—educators, scholars (not the same as "educators"), managers of institutions, including political institutions. What criticism can be enforced on any statement, on any supposed person? What is "wrong" about the subcultures, the drug-culture, even the mad? All is "permissive," but no one may grant permission. The "normal" is not an actuality but a statistic, as a psychologist said to me.

The classic virtues—courage, temperance, wisdom, justice—manifested a local control, a harmony of action and of utterance. The person appeared in his alliance with formal order, in tune with the universe. The universal was not another content of consciousness. It was both idea and the nature of things. In that order both person and world were defined and there allied. The resulting difficulty, and a persistent one, lay in the vanishment of the individual in the very world that his present integrity required. To avoid the rattle of incoherence, one joined the universe and then forfeited the authority of any here-and-now.

This has been the basis of the enduring problem of the will. In the nature of things, the will is not efficacious; yet apart from the nature of things, it dissolves into vagrancy. This is one of the longest stories on record. But the record shows the persistence of the quest for both an authoritative immediacy and a world.

On the one side, the proposal of local control gives offense to a universal order; on the other side, it offends an unordered stream of consciousness, which has no banks and may have none. On the totalitarian side, it offends theology and physics; on the radical empiricist side, it is patronized by psychology, an alleged science that repudiates the universal and can find none on its own terms. Anyone who attempts to control what I now do has nullified the agent. Anyone who "explains" what I now do on any terms other than those of the doing has obliterated the act.

It is the case that in terms of a totalitarian order local control is undiscoverable. It goes too far to call it even a "superstition," a term that reinstates a local control by alleging an aberration in an inerrant world where nothing is out of order. As for psychology, an error, superstition, or myth has the same status as any alleged truth, virtue, or reality. There nothing is out of order because *no* order can be asserted on its terms. Any order invoked by psychology is parasitic upon some nonpsychological regularity, including any supposed argument that addresses that point and any "facts" adduced in support. Ejected *via* the front door, an order is surreptitiously admitted by the back window.

The standard difficulty over the individual has been his loss of present and finite authority in the very order that he required to raise himself out of incoherence and nonentity. The Greeks were an individualistic lot and for that reason were also the discoverers of "hubris," a term still in use by expositors of tragic drama. The egotist forgot that the dice of the gods were loaded. Without order the pretense to presence collapsed. The person had to claim and to accept an alliance with a world represented in his acts and in his words. One spoke for oneself, yet only as one also spoke for a universal mathematics, logic, dialectic, and morality. They were not merely under the law, as were the barbarians and orientals. Logic was no authoritarian imposition, no alien regulator of what one might be properly saying. Aristotle had not come down from Olympus with tables of logical conformity. They were formalists but not conformists.

But therein appeared the difficulty and it has persisted. The present sought its validity in an order that extinguished it. And so we find stoics and, in the end, neo-Platonists. Infinity nullified the authority of the finite although invoked to clothe the finite with presence and authority. The discovery and fortunes of such insoluble opposition constitute the history of philosophy.

Until, and unless, we come to a basis for such radical distinctions, they will seem arbitrary and even nonsense. Do we "come" to such a basis or does it manifest itself in intimate ways? Yet we were, in fact, without it and somehow must come to it. What, then, is that immediacy that has generated and enforced these baffling distinctions?

I answer that it is the *actual*. But that is rather a dark saying. To give it some plausibility, consider the status of science as the accepted account of nature. It would, I take it, be admitted that science is a story told by man himself. There is no scientific revelation. Science, in fact, has not infrequently gone counter to views of nature associated with some revelation. Not only so; science shows its secular status in its self-correction. If science is wrong on any point, it is science that says so. On the whole we have stopped quarreling with its claims. The timetable of Archbishop Ussher has become a relic of a past age, a historical monument and venerable in that status, a statement "about" nature but not, like science, within nature. No one has been wrong in science except as his error neglects his own assumptions and procedure. We have enlarged upon Euclid and Newton without rejecting them. They were not unreasonable men, and they receive civil treatment from their successors and heirs. This self-correction of science reveals it as a truly historical mode of discourse. *Its past is its own doing.* In this respect it resembles the law and the rule *stare decisis,* where a past is modified on the same assumptions that had long ago been operative and are now more clearly apparent. In that way both science and the law are conservative. Both resist the discontinuous while embodying their own reformation.

To many persons science seems an esoteric speciality. Few would understand how men could arrive on the moon and then return to earth with awesome precision. And yet neither do we feel that nature as described by science has been foisted upon us. It seems continuous with common sense, common as accessible to any person who counts his fingers, tells time, takes a shortcut to his destination, or builds a fire. Science is the expansion of local control. To maintain that control is the energy that both allures and drives. Psychology speaks of drives or urges; yet no such drive but it ends in satiety, the cause of Schopenhauer's pessimism and the root cause of the passivity, helplessness, and victimization to which psychology has brought us. But if one counts and calculates, one has launched an inquiry that generates its own articulate infinity. To maintain local control we proceed. This is the evidence, and the sole evidence, both of personal presence and of a world that extends it.

This actuality is no mysterious relation of subject and object. It requires a vehicle of which the very distinction of subject and object is an inherent consequence. This vehicle is what I have called the midworld. We tell time apropos of a clock, measure in terms of a yardstick, calculate in terms of numbers manifested in beads on a wire, notches in a stick, notations, and words. These functioning objects are neither "perceived" in passivity nor "real," but actual, commanding, consequential. A man can be held only to his word. The rest is impotence. This word, whatever it may be, operates as a control, even as it also gives him presence and entails that order which is also his world. It is the medium in which the act appears that alone holds a person to what he has done. One is faithful to yardsticks, clocks, balances, numbers, words, monuments, institutions. Whatever is right or wrong, true or false, good or evil, ensues upon the authority of a self-critical utterance. The preservation of function is the maintenance of the functioning object, be it that body we call "the" body or any word spoken. The word is incarnate.

Any act proposing to be authoritative or even tolerable must invoke the inherent command of some utterance, of an actuality that regulates and enforces. The universal, the infinite, is the form of the actual. It takes no scholar to recognize that persons have been confident about themselves in so far as they have seen themselves allied with an infinity, a universal, a divinity. The novelty—as I take it to be—of the actual results from the mutuality of the finite and the infinite. The relation is dialectical, not logical. They are mutually dependent. They have a common sense. This is the energetic functioning object. I transfer the famous "entelechy" from objects of nature to yardsticks, clocks, words, and monuments. The eloquence is there. They are present, and they project what is not present but continuous with the present. Every word entails what is not now said, every space what is not now measured.

The common objects of experience wear a patterned dress, a uniform of place, time, class, quantity, and other "categories." Whether the uniformity of nature, if it can be asserted at all, is to be initial or eventual has been a troublesome and disputed problem. As initial this uniform has been regarded as *a priori,* not a derivative or resultant of the manifold particulars. As a generalization from particulars wearing no uniform whatever it has seemed not so much impossible as undiscoverable, no basis for generalization being available short of begging the question in one way or another. Expressions used to indicate this radical dualism are "form" and "content." Neither accounts for the other. They are in a state of divorce. As is usual in such cases, efforts are then made to bring them together. Various "theories" are proposed, all of which necessarily beg the question anew.

All structural or constitutional terms appear in some disarray. They conflict. Yet they cannot leave each other alone and their force depends on a recognition of a contrary. Philosophers have felt their integrity menaced by these contraries. Nonphilosophers avoid dealing with such inherent discordances. And yet, it is only in discord that any universal comes to notice in its urgent status. No universal is placidly obvious. The universal is a matter of integrity, not a matter of fact. It makes itself known as a menace to personal presence, to that local control that manifests any here-and-now whether past or present. Without inherent discord there is no composition, no tenacity of order in its various modes. Purpose and cause display their opposition only as we require both in order to go to the post office. The locus of both discord and composition is the actual.

I have found that professional philosophers demand either a completion without conflict, or else an atomization where no composition is possible and where discord and concord are both excluded. This, in various particular ways, marks the retreat to nihilism. Absolute order and absolute unorder are alike inarticulate, and the very words that appear to convey them are destroyers of both. Any word is a present and incorporate authority. The maintenance of that authority is the actual.

Any structural universe is incomplete. This is equivalent to saying that finitude is constitutional. The denial of that statement abolishes the actual, *the locus* of the finite. Nothing actual is either in complete order or in complete unorder. Unorder is not disorder. Disorder is a breach of order, a failure of local control. But where else is any failure to be found? I accentuate neither the positive nor the negative exclusively but the basis of both.

In order to free himself from a "block universe," William Jones would have no universe at all, but a pluriverse to which no limit could be set without forfeiting an uncontrolled "variety." But in pluralism there is no constitutional incompleteness because nothing constitutional can be allowed. On the other side, the complete constitutionalists have had notorious difficulty with any aspect of disorder, with evil, with failure, with life and death. I used to hear a lot about "the problem of evil." An absolute always in tune could not account for the "good tunes" of the Devil, which, allegedly, were *not* in tune with the universe. Literary critics tell me blandly that the Devil is the hero of *Paradise Lost*. What their world may be, the Devil only knows.

I do not find a constitutional incompleteness put forward in any of the "types" of philosophy. The only discourse that expresses it is history, where there is something less than a *fait accompli* and something more than atomistic unorder. That "less" and "more" is the act, the verb, the doing, a mystery in terms of knowledge. And so we have the spectacle of "theories" of history, as if we stood outside it, viewing it as another phenomenon, which is to be explained on some other basis, currently on a psychological basis, formerly on a theological basis. Any "explanation" of history is equivalent to the dissolution of a constitutionally authoritative present. It is the vanishment of the act in the alleged facts, of the agent in circumstances, or of all in an unordered "stream of consciousness." This is the silent world, where no voice is heard and no word is spoken. It is the denial of the incarnate word, the abyss of the "credibility gap" because no word, no utterance of any sort, declares the nature of things, where, in consequence, any world projected in utterance becomes a myth and the speaker an illusion.

The difficulty is not that *my* words go uncredited but that others refuse to appear in their own words. And surely where no word or act is one's own, none will be, or could be, attributed to another.

13

Facts and Artifacts

Now a few words about hammers and what may be their status in the incomplete universe: Tools seem not to be part of the "data." Hammers do not grow on trees. They are not "facts" but "artifacts"—a current term. A tool entails the addition or intervention of purposes where not all objects function as tools. It is supposed that we are aware of the "facts," then find them offering no satisfaction to our purposes, and that we thereupon devise tools or instruments that will modify that prior state of affairs.

Now that is a very risky vocabulary. There is the negative and also the universal in *"not all objects."* It seems an innocent phrase, yet it is loaded with assumptions that have been challenged as "metaphysical." "Purpose," too, is not a word accepted by all men. It smacks of local control.

That "prior state of affairs," the "facts," which are to be there without any intervention of our own, has also been heavily criticized. Where no purpose has intruded, the properties of such prior objects have been declared unknown. Some stones are harder than others, a fact discovered by attempting to split a stone with a tool to make an arrowhead. There is a passive empiricism where the facts are to be known *without* intervention of purpose or action; and there is also an empiricism that *requires* such intervention. Our research includes such active intervention. Modern science is of the latter sort.

Passivity has no tool. I take it that in Paradise there were no tools. It was after the expulsion that Adam delved and Eve span. He needed a spade, a tool, to accomplish a purpose. By digging, as I can testify, one learns something about the properties of soil—sandy, clay, loam, wet, dry, frozen. It begins to look as if that prior state of affairs, the facts, antecedent to the intervention of purpose, would be pretty hazy where nothing had been attempted, no tool used, no purpose controlling and urging. For all that, there persists the view that such a prior state of affairs in which no local control has intervened has been identified in the absence of tools.

This persuasion is related to the influential view that to "know" is to keep out of whatever one alleges to be so, that one can identify objects of a prior state of affairs before it occurs to one to make and use a hammer, a flint and steel, a needle, an arrow, a pot, a hut. None of that is to affect what one already knows and can say about the real facts. So, we claim to distinguish between the "facts" and the "artifacts."

Some say that the real facts, the prior state of affairs, must account for the alleged artifacts. The facts are to produce what we call artifacts. The latter are then threatened with disappearance in so far as the antecedent facts exhibit no purpose-control, no local control, no tools or instruments. The alleged artifact then becomes an illusion. In the dualistic alternative it becomes a rival reality, another sort of reality. This is then decried as a superstition by those who regard the real world as consisting only of facts devoid of artifacts. The superstitious cannot, however, be charged with allowing no credit to the facts. On the contrary, they usually assert them, but they also claim an ability to manage them with spades and hammers. The men of antecedent fact, of "real" fact where there is no artifact, deny the possibility of such external intervention and management. And one may notice that the alleged intervention does seem external on the premise of the "real" facts where no artifact operates as a *determiner* of the real facts.

There are plenty of people who talk suavely of artifacts but give no account of them in terms of the prior real facts.

Does the real world produce the Parthenon? Is the "stimulus" part of that real world, and the "response" also? And in terms of that real world what may a stimulus be? Are some of those real objects stimuli and others not, as some are sodium and others chlorine? I leave the question as rhetorical. But I must ask a further question: Can an artifact—no part of the real world—operate as a stimulus? Can what is *not* a real fact at all cause, or provoke, or generate a real response? Or, is an alleged response to an artifact as mythical as the imagined artifactual stimulus? If in terms of the real facts the hammer is an illusion, will not my response to it be equally so? Hammers and money do not grow on trees where trees are regarded as among the "real" facts, not as artifacts nor as specified by any intervening purpose.

I am sorry to bring such obscure words as "real," "stimulus," and so forth, into the discussion. But I did not invent them, and people who never doubt their solid common sense speak of "artifacts," products of "art" not of an artless nature. The innocent child is sometimes called "artless," not a fabricator, and not yet suspicious of the devices of others. But, as I pointed out in the general sketch of the incomplete universe, there is no escaping an account of the sort of world that can include the utterances, the affirmations, and denials that permit any world to be intelligible. In this case, a hammer seems indubitably "real," although *also* regarded as a "tool" or artifact. Yet these same people balk at any account of the real that is not independent of the artifact. It would be simpler to treat all artifacts as illusory. And so they must be, if the antecedent real facts are to be identified without benefit of art. Yet I have heard professors of art say that the painting, for example, assists in the perception of what is "really" there, as if without Grandma Moses one would miss seeing the farmyard, its house, barn, cattle, and farmers. It is strange to find artists discrediting the "literal," and yet making a point of the role of art in revealing "real" barnyards. By the same token, the hammer would be a factor in the discovery of what is really there, like the spade that brought information to Adam and to me.

The tenacity exhibited by people insisting that hammers are real while at the same time merely artifactual and not real at all—like any other tool—sets the stage for a problem. Why this tenacity? Why not settle the issue by a flat denial of the reality of any tool and so of the purpose alleged to be served by it? Why not say that anyone who treats a hammer as real merely advertises his illusion, his superstition? Some have said so.

In our frustrations we sometimes use hammers to smash an intruding artifactual object. Such are idols, phantasms, and we become iconoclasts like the Byzantines. So, too, we use words to destroy words, a common practice and the intellectual's delight. Moses, just down from Sinai, forbade graven images but, it seems, not also words, provided they were not his own. The word is also an artifact, or at any rate, any dictionary sort of word, the dictionary being only a history book. But while one can make some sense of smashing idols with a hammer (as the *Pietà* in St. Peter's was damaged), it is rather a sign of madness to vent frustration caused by the real world by assailing it with hammers. There the frustration becomes deeply radical. "Would not we shatter it to bits—and then remould it nearer to the Heart's Desire?" That real world is not our doing, and neither can we undo it. Striking at any reality with a hammer becomes absurd. And yet people suppose that they can crack a real stone with an unreal hammer, where that reality contains neither hammers, nor striking, nor a word for either, nor the purpose that strikes. Is one to suppose that one can interfere with the real world?

It is proposed, however, to strike a real stone with an unreal hammer, that is, with a hammer not discovered in the nature of things. Glaciers crack stones, but glaciers, like the stones they crack, are real, whereas the hammer is not. But this claim causes distress. The hammer, although only an artifact, is said to be a real hammer as well, it not being claimed that one can strike a real stone with an unreal hammer. We know about stones and subsequent to that knowledge devise a hammer to crack them. But what we know about stones is not to be dependent on hammers or other tools. It was clever of us to devise the hammer, given the hard stone as a prior real fact.

Magicians flourished when it was assumed that some device of our own could modify events. A spoken curse, or a blessing, was regarded as efficacious. Only a fortnight ago a competent man spoke to me about the favorable results of a blessing. In order not to offend him I said only that I was reluctant not to attribute his work and prosperity to some abilities and efforts of his own. I don't think I offended him. A gold ring worn at sowing brought a harvest of golden corn. A sword had magical properties, a peculiar "virtue" or power, as with Excalibur or Colada. An effigy of an enemy stuck with pins wrought his destruction. Examples are numerous.

We may regard magic as "primitive," as ignorance of nature. It is commonly accounted for in a negative way: they did not know any better; they lacked knowledge. We are sure that there is no connection between a gold ring and a good crop. But how is one to account for the shift from magic to knowledge? The medicine man could produce rain; so can we by seeding clouds. But there are eminent writers who have made a reputation by denying "necessary connections," that is, simply connections, in the supposed "data." In the absence of connections, it is no less magical to produce rain by chemicals than by the dance of medicine men. Pluralists want no necessary connections, fearing a "block universe," any universe at all. In fact science was regarded as necromancy and the scientist as in league with the Devil. Such a temper was plausible as recently as Goethe's Faust, who summoned spirits from the vasty infernal deep to aid his purposes. Is science only another sort of magic? And if it is not, how is one to account for the alleged transition from magic to science?

I have not seen this question addressed. On the one side, we say that there were animists and magicians; on the other side, that there never were any such "real" people. The real world has no magicians in it and never did have. I know a man who gives exhibitions of magic; is he "really" a magician or is he pulling my leg, not a magician at all, but a clever fellow exploiting my ignorance of what is "really happening"? Does he really saw the lady in half? Seeing is believing, is it not? There is "the sensible and true avouch of mine own eyes," a metaphysical article of the magician's creed. I once attended an exhibition of chemistry and saw colorless liquids change into blue, and vapors pouring from the bottle, just as in a magic show, a deliberate hocus-pocus to entertain the audience.

So, one says that the hammer is real. It drives a nail. Apart from the dubious claim that an artifactual hammer can drive an artifactual nail or crack a real stone, there is the question of the *connection* between the hammer and the nail or stone. Why not say that the hammer, or any tool, is a magical power, that it has the "virtue," the strength, the power to sink a nail or crack a stone? On what basis would one say more than that? Is there not a divorce between that real world and those artifacts? "Nature to be commanded must be obeyed," as Francis Bacon said; would one try to command that real nail or stone by swinging a hammer at it? Why not, rather, fall back on magic and settle for a magical hammer, which has the wonderful virtue of affecting a supposed prior and independent reality, just as wearing a gold ring effects an abundant harvest? A man might pride himself on being a more potent magician than his ancestors. We have advanced in magical practices. But as for any connection between the artifactual tool and those real objects, we are as much in the dark as Neanderthal man, or as Arthur was about the virtues of Excalibur. Fire is a potent magic and Prometheus brought it from Olympus. You could do wonderful things with fire, keep warm, for example, not a negligible effect up here in New England at twenty below. It is not claimed that Prometheus was a chemist who advanced the theory of phlogiston, let alone combustion.

The very word "artifact" seems a curious concoction, part "fact," part "arty"—like a centaur, part man, part horse, or like the cloud of Polonius, a camel, weasel, whale. Yet the word is used with assurance. Anthropologists and archaeologists say that they "find" artifacts, while physi-

cists find only the facts and psychologists engage in no
search whatever, short of invoking nonpsychological controls. Some years ago I spoke with an anthropologist who
assured me that history fell within the findings of anthro-
pology. Perhaps it would be admitted that the claim to
have found an artifact would not be made by any of the
natural sciences, that the centimeters–grams–seconds system discovers no fabrication, such as a hammer, and that
within its controls it arrives at no historical statement, as
Einstein himself declared. There is nothing arty in a test
tube: facts, perhaps, but no artifacts. So, if one alleges an
artifact as something found, one has made assumptions
about the controls of the findings and of the search. One
says that someone *made* an arrowhead or a hammer, someone acted and exercised a control not that of gravity or the
alleged speed of light. One might as well say that one
"finds" me going to the post office, a statement that would
raise eyebrows in intellectual circles emancipated from such
superstitious assumptions.

It is curious, too, that some artifacts are classed as
"myth," with the *Iliad,* the *Divine Comedy,* Chartres,
whereas tools do not suffer from that indictment. Yet the
tool, quite as much as the mythical object, is something
made, but for all that is not regarded as leading us into
illusion and unreality. On the contrary, it is supposed that
a tool keeps us in close rapport with the real world and its
real objects. I don't hear a man who drives a nail with a
hammer dismissed as a foggy fellow. I myself, a philosopher, have been asked by my wife to fasten a loose curtain
rod, for which operation I get a hammer and so gain status
as a sensible man not wholly lost in metaphysical vagueness, oblivious of the real world. My reputation with
neighbors was wonderfully improved because they saw me
digging with a spade, as if in so doing I was confessing to
the limitations of philosophy, brought back to the real
world of soil and tomatoes.

Spades, hammers, and such-like tools, although artifacts
and so hailed by anthropologists, seem to announce a commerce with the real world. Other artifacts—words, pen-

cils—seem to result in myth, as with poets and pictorial artists.

Truth is beauty, as the poet says. Or, is the truth closer to the sort of tool that effects a specific result, closer to the spade and hammer than to the pencil of poet or painter? And what about such tools—if they are tools—as yardsticks, clocks, numbers, which effect no specific change as does the hammer with which I fasten a curtain rod? You can perhaps imagine that I pricked up my ears when the professor soberly told me that mathematics was a tool— me, who dig with a spade and strike with a hammer for quite specific purposes and consequences, including a pleasing enhancement of my reputation as a sensible man, redeemed from academic vagueness.

It is assumed—not exactly admitted, but assumed—that tools are efficacious. And they are artifacts and so regarded. But neither are they magic, although magic also claims efficacy as above noted. Technology displaces magic. Why should it? It is because *the tool is continuous with the objects that it affects and is essential in the disclosure of the properties of specific objects*. Those properties are undiscovered as a wholly prior state of affairs to which a tool is subsequently applied. That would indeed be magic, an external influence upon an independent reality.

To put the matter in my usual and obscure terms: except in an actual world, any tool is magic.

Embroider on this for a bit. The hammer drives a nail. The nail, however, is no less an artifact than the hammer. Technique improves on a prior *operation*. The stone cracked by a tool has already been a tool, but less effective as a missile than an arrowhead split from that stone. Arrowheads, unlike Athena, do not spring from some Jovean brow. The priority assumed in the operation of an artifact is not a separately identified "reality," but a functioning with a measure of local control.

This is no more than to say that the effectiveness of a tool entails its specificity and also that of the object to be controlled by the tool. Any object so particularized has come to that status in consequence of a particularizing *pro-*

cess. Well, a long troublesome problem has concerned the mode of identifying particular objects, differentiating, classifying, and indeed, permitting one to speak of stones, wood, water as *objects* rather than as an alleged conjunction of miraculous "data," the conjunction itself undiscoverable in terms of such discrete data. This conjunction factor has long been a source of contention. When it has been insisted upon, one meets the formalists, who have said that such formal unification had an *a priori* basis. That basis was the universals. But what was their source and authority? "Content without form is blind"—words of Kant, but as old as the inception of controlled utterance. These universals have haunted the claim to "know," as when one says "this" object, a stone, *not* a piece of wood or bone. But *any* object is a "this," not a "that," quite as much as it is spatial, or one of many (quantity), or at a time. "This" is also a universal. But no "this" is "this" because it is red rather than sweet. Whatever operates to permit "this" object is not to be found in passive, discrete, unorganized data, in what we call the stream of consciousness. Passivity has no universal, neither a here-and-now nor a "this" nor a "that," a stone, which is not wood or bone, an *object,* not a content of consciousness—that very expression indefinable within its own boundless fluidity.

The universal has always made trouble for cognition. What are these Platonic "patterns," which haunt not only the infinities of space, number, time, cause, and so on, but *also the particular,* the "this" as equally inevitable? Either sort of universal has seemed an abrupt and unwarranted intrusion. You threaten me cognitively with a particular hammer, with that one in your hand. You say it is an object, a "real" object, and also a tool. On what basis am I to be impressed by such claims? Not only so; you say further that this here hammer is not only "real" but an "artifact" to boot. You do not claim to have any hand in the real world, but you say both that the hammer is "real" and also that your hand is in it, that you made it by art, and you made it out of a reality neither discovered nor affected by anything you do or could do. If I settle for that invulnerable reality, I then meet the claim that the alleged artifact is a superstitious illusion. On the other side, to the extent that I get confronted with artifacts—tools, monuments, words, dictionaries, arguments—the real becomes inscrutable, never putting in an appearance in terms of the arty control. History, for example, is arty both in its performance and narration, and its authority is then challenged by political science and by psychology, as it was formerly by theology.

I believe I do not exaggerate in saying that in so far as we live in an artifactual order we are under attack. The current cult is nakedness, back to nature. Let us shuck off these artificialities. Back to impotence. Power corrupts. The word uttered meets a jeer in its very pretentions to name or express any reality. The hammer, like the word, perpetuates illusion. A pity that these heralded artifacts were ever devised. One sees only too plainly what they have led to. Back to Paradise, where Adam needed no spade and nakedness was no shame, indeed, was not even perceived. In that Paradise there was no local control. It was introduced by the serpent, the cause of all our woe. Adam in passivity could not tell one tree from another.

On what basis would anyone object to my abjuring all artifacts, or to regarding them as great nonsense? "All Nature is but art, unknown to thee," but it is not one's own art. Nature is "real" just because it is *not* a tool, a device, an instrument of our particular purposes. Many and influential people have, however, considered nature "real" because it was also the evidence of a design, its very order addressed as proof of a Designer. But it was not our design. There has been this persisting persuasion that where there is order, as in nature, there is also a control in terms of an action, finite or infinite. Order without action, without controls, has had an implausible quality. And, to fall back on the record: where control has been denied, order also had no manifestation. Data embody no order. They reveal no necessary connections. The order of data if any, then becomes a speculation or "theory," an attempt to account for those data, their variety and genesis. Order is then regarded as an idea in the "mind," nothing more, nothing really there. As ordered, nature then has seemed an appearance only, a phenomenon not real at all. Much on that in the history of the problem.

Suspicious of such *a priori* order, we have not abandoned order. We propose controls and call them "postulates." Those postulates then control what we say is so in mathematics, physics, logic. When you studied geometry you met, on page one, "axioms, definitions, and postulates," the governing controls of what could further be said in that discourse. Well, postulates do not grow on trees. They are not brute facts. They are not "real," independent of anything anyone may do or say. Indeed, they have been revised and with such revision the very order of nature has been transformed. Such postulates are actualities.

But these famous postulates of science never tell you anything about particular tools—hammers, for example, or spades, and what is discovered in operations with such tools. Euclid says nothing about Adam's spade, or mine either. Nor does $E = MC^2$ tell anything about forks, knives, and spoons, buttons on your coat, or a zipper, all very handy tools, which you want, however, to be "real."

Well, we philosophers are badgered for speaking of reality, but plenty of people say with calm assurance that a reality precedes and accounts for such clever tools. They do not want that reality to be the consequence of such tools; they want the tools to be consequences of reality. The road is to run from reality to tools, a one-way street.

How to account for such bland assurance and impatiently stubborn insistence? The reality of a tool is not represented as a revelation, a brain storm, an intuition, a brute fact. Not at all. There is nothing to be done about reality. It is the world I never made and cannot unmake. Accept, submit, resign—if one goes so far as to allege what is really there and let there be no nonsense about having had a hand or a tongue in the discovery of what is really there. No verbs, if you please. Everybody tells what is really there, everybody, that is, except a philosopher. But *there* are the wind and the waves, the rocks and the planets, as anyone can see, provided, of course that one allows anyone to be *seeing,* a wretched verb, a superstitious intrusion, perhaps even accompanied by a saying "I see the moon resting on top of Mt. Williams" or "I go to the post office" or "I am going home to Elm Street by the light of the moon." "Do I dare to eat a peach?" And is walking on the beach less an intrusion? I was present at the Harvard Commencement when T. S. Eliot received an honorary degree for saying such things. The behavioral scientists must have had amusing thoughts, so to say. But I am not at all confident that Eliot ever actually wore white flannel trousers or any other sort, let alone walked in them. "Unreal City." "Shanti."

I will now say that the tool is the *particular actuality* on which the discovery and specification of all "real" particulars depend. The particular object—wood, stone, water—is "perceived" apropos of some means of dealing. Use a spade and learn about soil; use a saw and learn about wood, the grain and the cross grain; use water to learn about fire and fire to learn about water. Until fire is made and put out, it is a miracle. Until made it is not "real" rather than imaginary or neither. We do not control the real world; we call an object "real" apropos of the control that *particularizes* it. Particularity and reality are complementary, or as I might say in an incautious moment, dialectical and constitutional. I repeat, however, for the sake of the contrast, that no particular object is passively "perceived." The psychological has no token, no determinative actuality, no incorporate purpose. No tool without purpose, no purpose without tools. We don't get the better of reality with a tool; we identify it in its particulars.

I must admit a weariness in this crying up of artifacts only to meet charges of superstition and myth in so far as I credit the deed and mention a midworld, which is neither appearance nor reality but the source of their distinction, the actual. The tool of any sort is the medium of the particular act and particular object. Any reality not a brain storm passes through a medium. Short of a tool any purpose lacks specificity. The assault on purpose-control is the nihilism of all particulars.

Well, here I am saying a word for particulars. Since I am a philosopher, I am expected to speak only in terms that would leave particulars a mystery. Sensible men deal with particulars; philosophers try to get rid of them, and some have indeed belittled hammers and spades or, at least, have been puzzled by their status. Others have emphasized the particular at the expense of the other universals. And some have regarded both as illusions of an alleged stream of unordered consciousness where even the consciousness has no definition. I submit for consideration that the tenacity that wants hammers to be both artifactual and real is the sign of a *threat* to any particular reality in the absence of the determinative tool.

Of course, the tool's status as a universal, essential for the complementary universality of the particular, modifies the pragmatic status of the tool as an alleged utility employed against a prior reality for the satisfaction of an alleged desire. I am saying that a tool has an *intrinsic* allurement as a medium of discovery of all particular objects. *There* is the source of the tenacity with which people cling to artifacts. Tools enlarge purposes, they do not merely satisfy some vagrant desire and leave one with a Schopenhauerean satiety. I submit that the numerous persons who equip a basement with tools would not rest with "practical" explanation and justification. They learn something. They get a grip on particulars. Tools are also demanding. It is the barbarian who treats an auto as an instrument of a vagrant purpose, and it is a stupid fellow for whom a clock is merely now and then useful. I suppose that Einstein looked to see if it was supper time, but it was not in that way that he made his reputation.

Ah well, I have proposed some "categories," all based on the actual and the midworld. Here I am saying that the maintenance of purposes is an act of will, quite as much as not using a yardstick as a tool or supposing that it butters any parsnips. We can't let go of the purposive order—not just to make some butter (which the physician advises one not to eat anyhow) but to find out what butter may be. A tool is also an adventure.

Just the same, tools require numbers and yardsticks, the

nonparticular universal. Functioning objects and functional objects differ as will differs from purpose, the constitutional from the particular, or the structural from the occasional. Hammer, saw, needle are indistinguishable in the order projected by space, all being spatial—substantial, qualified, classified, and so forth. Not so with yardsticks, clocks, words. I have two hammers, a claw-hammer and a ball-peen hammer; they differ in function; two yardsticks are indistinguishable in so far as their functioning determines spatial quantity. The disclosures of yardsticks and clocks are in terms of a universal; the outcome of hammers is a particular. The functioning object yields no "terminating satisfaction"; the functional object accomplishes an end result. (If I remember, it was John Dewey who wanted "terminating satisfactions." But I am not now going to elaborate on the absurdity of proposing "instruments" on a psychological basis.)

The distinction of tool from functioning object is *made.* It is made in utterance and nowhere else. Nor was the distinction clear from the start. It developed. It was historical. Many have not yet made the distinction and are uneasy over it. I say that I make it, but I do not say I made it all by myself, as if it were a bolt from the blue, a revelation vouchsafed to me. Not at all. How did I become aware of it? It was in the talk. There was a telling of time, a measuring, calculating, inferring. And there were hammers, so named. People often spoke in terms of universals, as when they told the time or alleged a cause or said I couldn't have my cake and eat it too, and put me down when caught doing so. But I deny that all by myself I invented clocks or grammar or logic; no, not even hammers. I did invent a cement mixer when wanting to build a wall, but even so there was the consideration of saving time and of making it of a size. I used nuts and bolts, but had not invented them. So you see I am really a modest man.

The pure sciences are also the pure action. What does one "know" about any purposive need or result because $7 + 5 = 12$? Where will it get you? as people say. The "practical" gets you to a particular result.

It burst upon men that the practical, the "tool," had entailed the universal. That was a late, and a reflective, discovery. It brought continuity and infinity. It brought words. There is no hammer until there is a *word* for it. The tool is an un-self-conscious actuality. There are no tools in nature or in the psychological stream of consciousness. Within the solar system there is no tool, nor within the nervous system.

The willful and the purposive are dialectical. Purposes find expression only in universals, as in going to Jericho, a distance, and going today, not yesterday, a time. No arrow or spear was of a length, of a weight, of a hardness and toughness not present in some materials. In fact, purpose-control was *not identified explicitly* until confronted by the universal and willful. Moralizers still disparage purposes and leave their own as disreputable as another's. So they also lose any will of their own and call themselves virtuous in consequence.

The functioning object is the *formal* constituent of the functional object, which is the *content* of the actual. Yardsticks, clocks, words are apropos of purposes, while purposes invoke the universal. Where nothing has the *status* of a tool, no general order is suggested; and where there is no general order, the tool vanishes. Technology falls back on physics, but the occasion for physics is the technically controlled act or problem. Clock-time serves no purpose, but no purpose can be declared without it.

Form has been explored more than the particular. The world—if there is to be a world—comes dressed as a general order. It wears a uniform, especially a mathematical uniform. Particulars have lacked similar attention. They seem abrupt, in contrast with the continuum of any map. And they seem out of control, not corollaries of any general order. Because you can calculate and measure you do not, in consequence, know the height of Greylock.

So, I have had the difficult problem of bringing particulars also into a midworld or into the actual. Particulars seem unconnected with doing. They are called data, essentially miraculous and yet unescapable. They have been associated with the senses, we speak of a sensual man with disapproval. He is as vagrant as his data, undiscoverable as a person and individual.

The sensualist is all body. "The body is the coffin of the soul" (Socrates). But it is also "the temple of the Holy Ghost" (Christianity). We get particulars through the body and the senses. We need eyes and ears. You need them even to measure the height of Greylock or to count your money, or to hear Homer sing, or to read the Bible. What, then, has been the cause of a persistent ambiguity over the role of the senses?

The cause, I have been saying, is the failure to recognize the body as a functioning object. The phrase *"the* body" is nonsense where *the* body is *a* body. Nobody finds *his* body as *a* body. Where, among bodies—sticks, stones, water, stars—am I to find my own? Where, indeed, would I get the idea of looking for *my* body? Science has no way of authorizing the phrase "the body" or "my body." I did not come upon *my* body when I had a course in chemistry. The textbook made no reference to it, that is, to me as embodied.

Yet that instruction did assume that I was there in the body, looking, smelling, handling test tubes and Bunsen burners, that I was to be careful to keep certain acids or gasses away from hands and eyes. I wore an apron in order to protect my clothing. Rather spooky, a ghost in a laboratory! Yet not a pure ghost, but an embodied one who could set the place afire or cause an explosion and this not by some hocus-pocus but by what I was alleged to be doing or not doing.

So, I have been crying up what I call local control. *The* body appears in that capacity, as actual, not as factual; as functioning, not as accidental datum; as a doing to which all finding is derivative; as inseparable from the verb and the present active participle. I have claimed that nobody can distinguish seeing from hearing or the eye from the ear, apart from action, from the control inherent in look-ing, a verb, rather than hearing. By themselves, all quali-ties are discontinuous and unrelated. It is in the control—

turning the head, and so on—that visual qualities get distinguished from the auditory and associated with each other. I never read a book on psychology that accounted for a *group* of qualities called visual. That grouping is in functioning, not in the data. In fact, the men of data resist any controlled grouping or connection. The connection of red with blue is in the control of looking, a verb. Passivity has no visual qualities as distinguished from any other sort.

Of such local control *both* universals and particulars are the inherent consequences. What we call *the* environment is the projection of local control and in the absence of such control both person and world fall into chaos.

I state a consequence: matter, that mysterious stuff, never seen, evading all perception, an irrational surd for all pure formalists, now has status in the actual, in the functioning object, in a yardstick, in the body, in the seeing eye.

14

Matter

A person or society is called "materialistic"; others are seen as "spiritual." The former term is derogatory, the latter laudatory. The two have been at loggerheads, or have been said to be.

The Greek sages should be seen as men of "mind" rather than of "spirit." In terms of mind, both matter and spirit were, and have remained, in disrepute. The mind was uncomfortable with *entities;* it sought relation and order. Mathematics might apply to objects but was not generated by them. The mind "comprehended," unified, universalized, or, better, was *allied* with the order of experience, with the formal and rational. The sage was no scatterbrain. The senses and the experience limited to them, originating in them, did not disclose the nature of things, the *phusis.* The distinctive quality of man was reason and so the urge to join the ordered world. Partialities, if understood, required totality. Change, if not helter-skelter, required the permanent and invariable, the patterns fixed in heaven, the unmoved mover, the One of Plotinus.

The result was that some story of the *dispersal* of the one into the many was called for. This, in various guises, was "emanation," the process by which the unity diversified itself. Accounts of that process may strike us as fantastic, but that such an account *be provided* was necessary if the particular, the manifold, the relational, the finite, the unorganized and incomplete, were to be rescued from incoherence. Except as the manifold was to be the manifestation of a unity, it could attain no unity. The "nature of things" was their unity. Physics writes equations of invariant and universal order, where any change is absorbed into the constant and does not stand by itself.

The mind was then required to return to that unity that had produced the diversity. The vehicle of diversity was matter, the body and all other bodies, all other objects. The body was an obstacle, and the individual soul, as rational, was to lose itself in the universal mind, to see all things "under the aspect of eternity" as Spinoza rephrased an ancient necessity. Pure reason has nothing to reason about, no incomplete diversity to be held together. This is "the flight of the alone to the Alone." Only as alone could we expect to join the Alone. The aloneness was *the same* as our participation in the universal. A spark of the divine resided in the individual, graphically represented in the finger of God touching Adam in the famous Sistine fresco.

Christianity declared that the "Word was made flesh." It is the mystery of the incarnation. But it remained a mystery. Now, I am a Christian in so far as the incarnation is the actual. Up to a point Christianity gave authority to the actual. It did not *universalize revelation*. But I find the steady power of Christianity in its claim that—*at least once*—the absolute was embodied and took on mortality. That was neither Greek nor Jew. But that was the "detonator" scanted by Constantinople, but not by Rome. Yet: "My kingdom is not of this world."

There are curious features, however, such as "I believe in the resurrection of the dead"—as if *the* body were of some cosmic standing; as if, without *the* body, something important had been omitted—a curious insistence in a "spiritual" world.

To this day the emancipated intellectual hesitates to say that he lives on Elm Street. He is a man of mind, a universalist of sorts, but not of a formal sort. If the ancient universalist was not ready to settle as Athenian or Roman, it was because the ordered universe was not Athenian or Roman. The radicals of the ancient world were formalists. The Olympian gods were not threatened by anarchy but by a non-egotistic order, which made the world intelligible. I venture that it was Plato as much as anyone who overthrew Olympus. Charges of impiety were brought against Anaxagoras and Socrates.

The modern universalist is not a formalist. All formal universals have been attacked, not excepting causality and matter. There are no necessary connections. We are pluralists, a sophisticated term for anarchy. No limit can be set to variety without circumscribing it and so abandoning its primacy. The word today is "data," where every datum is discrete and miraculous. Ours is a cult of passivity. We are "open minded" and receptive. But no one dare say that he has a mind of his own. That is regarded as equivalent to a closed mind, credulous, superstitious, arbitrary, and, worst of all, pitifully victimized, a plague in its demands on oneself and an irritation to others. Modern universalism is passive, which is the same as nonformality. It is sometimes overlooked that while ancient formalism led to a completeness of absorption in the unenvironed whole it also entailed an *energy* and an endless adventure. Name any formality—space, time, cause, implication—and you have named a process rather than a static arrest. Socrates proposed to go on inquiring, to go on talking with the wise, with Minos and Rhadamanthus; the Platonic enthusiasm was erotic, a middle condition between poverty and plenty. "Awake my soul, stretch every nerve, and press with vigor on."

But this formal energy did not apply to the unenvironed whole. The absolute was not categorized, was not maintaining itself in a tenacious evolution of any formal order, forever incomplete and problematic. God was not to be described in any formal terms. He was not anthropomorphic. God could be approached not on *our* terms, but only on *his own,* a view essential also to the Christian doctrine. And yet, that the unmoved mover could be proposed or imagined at all was the *consequence* of those formalities, which suggested, but *did not attain,* completion. An ordered totality came into view only with an ordered present with which the person was identified. Pythagoras was not describing the catastrophic data or the stream of consciousness. Mathematics has a career, a history, because it is an energy, not a datum.

The long attack on formalities, that is, on universals, was an attack on the energies without which no universal could be described. It resulted in the cult of passivity. It was the surrender of control. This is the *pseudo-universalism* of the formless. No datum can be criticised as false or illusory in the absence of an assumed order, which no datum can supply. The universal is not a datum, nor a datum a universal. It may be said that the data of our natural science are not the data of psychology. The former are controlled as when one measures with yardsticks, clocks, balances; the latter are discrete, episodic, miraculous. Neither are they bound by controls nor do they enforce consequences. There is no psychological procedure for generating psychological data. Procedure is syntactic. Passivity has no procedure. It has no negations. A negative invokes an order, which passivity cannot generate in its absolute resignation. But passivity is not out of control; it is neither out of control nor under control.

The persistent difficulty of the ancient world appears in the conflict between reason as an energy and the unenvironed whole to which reason led. Reason was at once universal and therefore totalitarian, and yet incomplete. It proposed infinities that were procedural and not static. But if reason led to a totality it was because any rule of reason—or of its failure—had *presumed* a universal order. What warrant was there for claiming that *every* event had a cause, or that one increasing purpose runs? The question, however, was not whether such a rule could or could not be responsibly discovered but what could possibly suggest a warrant, a rule, a universal, a control. Radical empiricism operates by easing us out of prior assumptions of universal scope. It is all done very decently, as when Berkeley asks very politely what one could possibly mean by "matter." It puts in no appearance. There used to be plenty of talk about "body and mind," but "body" meant a recognizable *object,* such as that peculiar body called the "organism"— very detailed in its description. But matter *per se,* the supposed common stuff of organisms and sedimentary rocks, never came into focus.

If there was no talk "about" matter, it may then be suggested that the reason lies in an *inability* to talk about it. So soon as there is talk "about," there is an object, something peculiar, distinguished by qualities, a "this," not a "that," classified in some way, relational, at a place and time, caused or causing, perhaps perceived or perhaps an illusion. But there was no description of matter. I remember a professor who said that all knowledge was "description," this in the interest of getting rid of necessary connections. Description is said to be one of the four modes of prose discourse, but what one describes is the Grand Canyon or a violet by a mossy stone, in any case an object made peculiar by the description itself and distinguished from others in that account. As material, however, the Grand Canyon is no different from the shy violet. There are men of the visual arts who say that the painting shows us what was "there," as if the *re*-presentation were a factor in any presentation. But there is no picture of "matter," whereas Apelles shows us fruits, and Grandma Moses a farmyard. One cannot talk "about" matter. So soon as there is any sort of talk, verbal or pictorial, there are only particular objects. It appears that matter is not *re*-presented, because it is never *presented.* That, of course, is the claim that put Bishop Berkeley in the books.

So, I say bluntly: "Don't talk to me about matter; you cannot talk 'about' it."

In the current emphasis on "linguistic," the residual problem is what one is to say about *syntax,* as when one talks in terms of "how many," "where," "when," "for what reason," "to whom," "on what occasion." Matter eludes syntax. Without difference there is no composition. But matter is *the same* in all its alleged guises or disguises. The impersonal pronoun "it" has no denotation when applied to matter. The ancients had a point when they, or some of them, saw matter as "nonbeing." They said it eluded mind. One begins to wonder how the word "matter" could have entered the vocabulary. But I find it in my dictionary. You propose to hit me with a hammer; *that* will show me "matter"! Nonsense. All I get—if you allow the personal pronoun—is sensation; or are you abandoning psychology? "Whatever is in the mind was first in the senses." And that is all you have to go on. There is no specific quality for matter, as red, sweet, hot, and so on. I used to hear about the "specific energy" of nerves; you don't see with your nose or smell with your eye. Matter is *not* specific. *No matter what* you see, hear, taste, or smell, it isn't "matter." Such distinctions are "immaterial," as the lawyers say. In fact *all* distinctions are "immaterial." That is what all the advocates of "mind" had been saying. An ideally complete syntax is pure mind, or pure spirit, or pure act. Matter has been left behind, or was never there. The unmoved mover does not go to the post office, just in time, by the clock, to make the last collection.

It begins to look as if "matter" might be a universal, like them lacking in specificity, as with space, time, quantity, cause, and many more. But while all universals have been attacked as neither content nor as derivable from atomistic "data," they have had great appeal, if only as "presuppositions" or as "postulates." Nobody abandons them, that is, nobody who counts his fingers, or goes from Jerusalem to Jericho, or minds his *p*'s and *q*'s, or alleges that someone else has not minded them. The senses do not make sense or talk sense. They do nothing and say nothing. But if matter be a universal, it differs from others in its total lack of syntactic structure. One can say that the world is spatial, temporal, quantitative, causal, because such formal universals project a world. They give shape and order. They articulate modes of infinity. But matter has no shape, structure, form, order. It is a blank to the mind, an "undifferentiated homogeneity," as it has been called in sesquipedalian terms. It is the inarticulate infinity. At the same time it haunts the formal universals, which attempt to make order out of the unordered and derive their prestige and attraction from that unifying power. The formal universals have been at odds with the very state of affairs on which they depend for their appeal. Disorder entails some order. A disorderly room is still a room, different from another room. Disorder is recognizable and articulate; unorder is not so. Disorder begs the question.

The strange tenacity of the idea of matter is inexplicable except as it is no less absolute than its formal rival and, indeed, essential to the pretensions of that rival.

It may well be that the key to a future view of man and the world will be in the establishment of "matter." It has been a constant and haunting item throughout the history of philosophy, but it has rarely, if ever, been accorded a *constitutional* role.

Philosophy appeared with the universal, with geometry and number, with an order regarded as mental or psychic. From the beginning matter has seemed an alien. The material world had to be accounted for on some other basis. I cannot disregard the enduring pervasiveness of the creation story: the material world was derivative.

Because derivative it remained less than quite "real." In fact its very presence was a mystery. Not only Job, but everyone else, too, has laid his hand upon his mouth.

We hear today of "alienation." What is the basis of that feeling? How would one overcome it? Its basis is the mystery of the material world, a world I never made. Its cure is seen as an evasion of that world, its dismissal as constitutional with one's supposed presence. Since it is no longer God's world, the evasion takes other forms—permissiveness, hysterical ecstasy, drugs, "consciousness expansion," "don't fence me in," the excellent thought that freedom is where you have nothing to lose—a thought sung by a rock-singer, a drug addict, and a suicide. Such alienation is not psychological but more fundamental.

Philosophers get no acceptance because they are regarded as dealers in thought, theory, hypotheses, speculation. Very well; lay all that aside, and the result has been the old mystery of Job. But Mrs. Job had an answer too; it was "Curse God and die." Why not, on the premises? She was "alienated."

Where, in the history of philosophy, does one find a claim for the *embodied* thought? "The philosopher studies to die." The senses deceive. Radical empiricism, escaping from "theory," escaped in equal measure from the material world—a point not recognized by the admirers of David Hume.

On this point I am attracted by the communists and their "dialectical materialism." They are the only modern men who give a constitutional role to matter. For that reason they find hostility from all religions, for which the material world is derivative. They are not "spiritual." But neither are they radical empiricists. Of course, I view a "dialectic" of matter as nonsense. But so do I view a dialectic of the disembodied as nonsense. The communists want history without actuality. But they *do* want history and make a bow to Hegel. But then, Hegel also discounted the actual. The owl of Minerva was a spectator, not an actor. That bird did not fly through the air nor seek its prey. It was a wise bird. "The less he spoke, the more he heard; why aren't we like that wise old bird?" Communists cannot abide the actual, the person present, because he is a walking, speaking, counting, singing man. They want history, but no act. But who does want the act?

It is notable that when one turns to science, supposedly the antagonist of the mental or spiritual, one does not come upon "matter." One has uniformities and equations expressed in nonmaterial terms. There are numbers, grams, seconds, centimeters—all "units of account," not material objects. Matter is as unknown to science as it was to the passive perceptions of Berkeley. Even the ancient atom has drawn suspicion as a "real" thing, and it has been called a useful "hypothesis." Like God, it is observed only in its effects or workings and eludes direct observation. There is no end, it seems, to atoms, sub-atoms, and sub-sub-atoms. Of course there isn't.

Science has *not* provided us with matter. It evokes a non-scientific revelation and says that the law of gravity "fits" all objects, a falling stone or the moon. But it does not account for the stone or the moon or for any particular object. All fade into illustration of uniformities.

This explains the reluctance of science to allow *the* body—the unique, individual, functioning, and *materialized* actuality. That is a controlling factor in "behavioral science."

As derivative, matter is a mystery; as scientific, it is undiscoverable; as control of consciousness, it is not even an illusion or possible fiction. Theology, physics, psychology give no constitutional place to matter.

Why, then, not abandon the idea? What, indeed, is there to abandon? What does one lose if one simply drops matter—a notorious blank, a darkness, indefinable, limitless, indistinguishable from nothingness? I think it must be admitted that the persistence of the idea is very odd. Matter is *nothing that is*—whether as supposed object, or as content of consciousness. It always recedes. It *never* appears. Mind, thought, spirit have been spoken of scornfully on that basis: they do not appear. If we then abandon them, why not also matter, and for the same reason? One can account for illusions when they have some shape, as when a man fancies himself Napoleon, or persecuted. One can account for errors when they particularize. But how account for an absolute illusion or error?

The loss in losing matter is the loss of the actual. I cannot say in theological, physical, or psychological terms "I am going to the post office." The manifestation, the appearance of matter is in the actual. Matter must be *made* manifest.

The same actuality is also the manifestation of mind or spirit. They have the same root. Deny or overlook the actual, and then one loses *both* matter and spirit. All that is consequent on the midworld and the functioning object.

The problem has been long discussed and the "solutions" are named: interaction, dualism, parallelism, reduction. But neither matter nor spirit makes itself manifest.

I propose, then, to make matter a philosophical universal, and so constitutional, not an alien, not an object to be talked "about," any more than mind or spirit are to be talked "about," or (for that matter) zero, infinity, or finitude.

I marvel at the Christian idea of the incarnation. It is

amazing. Yet it proved popular and has so continued. I am proposing that any utterance has that quality of revelation. A yardstick or a clock is a metaphysical actuality, an incarnate power. Until the word was made flesh, it had no actuality.

15

A Few Outlines

i. Language

Thesis: Language is the form of activity, not of objects. There is language where there is action. There are objects where there is action, *not* merely where there is "thought" or experience.

(1) There are no signs without meaning.

(2) There is no meaning as an object.

(3) There is meaning in the sign, which is both subject and object.

ii. Symbols

(1) All knowledge occurs through symbols.

(2) The self and the object are hidden, and to neither is there a direct approach. This is why there has been so much dispute over the propriety of alleging knowledge of the self and of objects. The self, some say, can be known only through objects, while objects, some say, can be known only through the perceiver and his data.

(3) Our knowledge of neither self nor nature is direct. It is in artifacts and institutions that we learn about man. Nature is known only through its symbolization in words, instruments, and formulated laws or hypotheses.

(4) Symbols are objects but are not accounted for in the terms of physics.

(5) Symbols are objects that control the exploration of objects, as in words, the instruments of physics, etc.

(6) All empiricism operates through symbols.

(7) The original symbol is the body and its organs. Unless one stands off from one's body and alleges a disembodied mode of experience, one cannot quite objectify the body. It is the original instrument and actuality of experience. The body is not a physical body or object, but the condition of all knowledge of bodies. It is not known as body *directly,* but only as part of a region to which it belongs and with which it is continuous. Nor are other bodies known apart from the activity of one's own body.

(8) Theories of knowledge usually work on bodies in nature, roses, tables, etc. Why not on one's own? This would suggest that other bodies represent an abstraction and are not the original situation of knowledge.

(9) Psychology has no instruments that define *other* bodies. It can only tell how, in terms of one's own body, the other bodies get taken into account.

(10) Thus, the body is, like a symbol, both object and the condition of objects.

(11) The second type of symbol is the artifact. But especially the *pure* artifact, the functioning object. All knowledge of objects moves through them and employs them. No object is otherwise known. All objects are denoted through symbols; all hypotheses expressed and tested through them.

(12) No question of ostensive definition occurs until symbols of another sort are assumed. One can point only in answer to a question. Note, too, that all questions occur via symbols; all uncertainty and confusion lies there. We are uncertain of objects only as we are uncertain of the symbols through which objects get defined, articulated, and so made continuous with other experience.

(13) Pointing implies a context. It is no substitute for symbols, but an evidence of the relation of symbols to a situation involving the prior identification of object, one's body, and the symbols that allow question and ambiguity.

(14) No pointing makes sense apart from exclusion. The

question "What do you mean by a rose?" assumes that one can identify other objects apropos of discourse, and the pointing and the question are meaningless apart from the limited universe of discourse in which they occur.

(15) Where no specific object is in question, one can't point; for example, one can't point to nothing or to cause or to purpose or to pointing. One can't point to functions or to universals, negatives, errors, etc. These are the conditions of pointing.

(16) Pointing is not, then, another object. It implies an artifactual context.

(17) Nor is the arm that lies along a direction a "pointer," where the arm is only object. The limbs of a tree don't "point," because they are not artifacts.

(18) Pointing implies the functioning of the arm, hand, or finger. It implies that these are not just objects.

(19) A passive empiricism cannot avail itself of pointing. In passivity there are no objects, no definition of objects via pointing, that is, via one's body, its organs, its explorations, its functioning.

(20) Pointing is invoked in those philosophies that separate data from form and order, as in Ayer. For in passivity there is always the residual mystery of what the body is. It is a mystery that *appears* to be over what one has in *mind,* where the mind is not already public. But this is the fallacy of passivity. In passivity one has nothing in mind because there is no mind in passivity. The separation of order from data prevents one from saying "What did you just *now* have in mind about the object over *there,* or about what *sort* of object, or about the interesting, colorful (*vs.* auditory), large, moving object?"

iii. Signs

(1) There can be no absolutely general theory of signs, for a theory of signs does not include the theory and the expression of the theory.

(2) The reason for this derives from the impossibility of treating signs as objects. No sign can be studied as an object.

The study of objects is the subject matter of physics. The relations between objects are the relations of the categories (space, time, cause). To treat a sign as an object is to lose it as a sign. Thus, the sign "Rooms" that I see out my window is probably a piece of wood with a coating of white lead and pigment reflecting light rays. To study the wood, the white lead, the pigment, or the light source is not to study the properties of signs but the properties of wood, lead, and light.

(3) Theory is an organization of objects, a unification of variety. The sign is not an object. Hence there is no *theory* of signs.

(4) There is no empirical way of understanding signs. Empiricism operates upon the specific, upon particulars. But signs are not particular. Anything can be a sign, but not anything can be gold or radium, moving at thirty miles per hour, 212° F., one yard long.

(5) Since signs are not a special class of objects, the meaning of a sign will not be found by observing any such class.

(6) What denotes no particular object is either nonsense or an element in order. Thus the number 1 denotes no particular object, nor does zero, or −2, or "not" or "thus" or "now," etc. Thus "sign" is a term of order and hence *a priori*. In a radical empiricism (Hume) there are no signs because there is no order nor any way of defining order, nor any way of denying order.

(7) Signs can be looked for (a) as a sort of object, (b) as a specific relation among objects, (c) as a relation between subject and object, (d) as the most general name of any type of order among objects. Thus, there are relations of predication and relations of cause. Each type has its sign in each particular or individual case. But the idea of a sign covers all possible types of interpretation of all possible data.

(8) Essentially, the sign is the datum. Any datum is a sign. The special relations of the datum to other data—physical, chemical, psychological, historical—are all interpretations of the original sign. Thus, an account of signs reduces to an account of the various types of order.

(9) The assertion that S is a sign of P may be true or false. This truth or falsity is the place of S and P in some context of special order. The sign must declare which order it appeals to. Thus, a cloud is a sign of a storm, or a sign of Jehovah, or a sign of being hungry, or a sign of the decline of the Roman Empire. Thus, a sign must appeal to some universe of discourse or to some type of order. But signs in themselves have no special order. The order of signs is order in principle, that is, the structure of the necessary.

(10) No sign denoting a universal factor of objects or of experience possesses behavioristic occasions. What is involved in all occasions expresses no particular occasion. And if there is no account of factors present in all occasions, then there is no relation of any particular occasion to any other. For that relation—even the relation of particularity itself—occurs in terms of order. Thus, the relation of events in nature is space, time, cause, quantity, etc. A particular has relations only because it is defined through order. Were it not so defined, no assertion of relation would be demonstrable, for no restrictions on pluralities would be involved.

iv. The Cognitive Datum

The more I think of it, the more it seems that the idea of the (1) *cognitive datum* is important.

Data occur apropos of a quest—or question.

But the quest must be more than psychological; the interest involved, more than purposive. The datum when cognitive must be disinterested—*the (2) disinterested datum.*

The epistemology of innocence is based on the neutral datum. It is (3) *neither interested nor disinterested.*

The disinterested cognitive datum occurs apropos of a quest, but apropos of a disinterested quest. This requires that the quest be controlled by some nonpsychological factor. A nonpsychological factor is one that is already objective, not merely an idea.

The datum that is cognitive must occur apropos of a particular object. It seems that data when dissociated from particulars are only appearances. Whether they are cognitive is not settled by their occurrence. They may be merely mental, or *neither* mental nor in nature. What makes the datum cognitive is its appearance in a context already said to be cognitive. What makes it disinterested is its being nonpsychological.

The combination of (a) cognitive, (b) disinterested, and (c) particular occurs apropos of the symbol. The temperature at 8:00 A.M. this morning is read from a thermometer. The datum is cognitive because it pertains to nature; it is disinterested because it occurs apropos of an instrument; it is particular because it is about this morning's air in Williamstown.

The *a priori* as form has no heuristic value. Pure math and pure logic determine no particulars. They lead to no data. Hence, (4) *the cognitive datum occurs apropos of an order possessing heuristic value.*

No purely formal order has such value. Heuristic value for particulars requires the symbol or instrument that is already part of the region in which the datum is to be looked for and encountered. (5) *No symbol is heuristic until it is also in nature and sensory.*

It is the sensory instrument or symbol that determines particulars. This it can do only as it actually occurs among other particulars of which it is the actual order. A yardstick measures a piece of ground or the distance between two particular objects.

(6) *Thus, the heuristic symbol determines particulars with respect to that property which they share with the symbol.*

Nor do particulars have such properties apart from the symbol. (7) *The symbol specifies and makes particular an object already in the same order as the symbol.* Thus one does not use a yardstick to tell time, or a clock to tell place. On the other hand, the yardstick can tell place only where place is already assumed, but *not* in its determination.

Thus, symbols function in a region indeterminate with respect to particulars. (8) *Symbols assume the indeterminacy of particulars with respect to their specific mode of order.*

(9) *No indeterminate region is established apart from the symbol.*

The separation of form from content leaves the content

indeterminate and its formal composition arbitrary. (*10*) *Logical empiricism is a theory of absolutely indeterminate content.*

The historical function of all forms of radical empiricism is to make plain the incompetence of such empiricism for the discovery of particulars. (*11*) *Its historical function is to raise the problem of the cognitive datum.* What gives the datum cognitive status is its capacity to determine particulars in one of their modes. Thus, radical empiricism has been the occasion for the necessity of actuality and function.

Empiricism, beginning as an emphasis on content, and as a reaction against formal orders without heuristic value, ended by encountering its own heuristic impotence. The true difficulty over empirical content is not that of its formlessness, but of its failure to provide the very particular determination that occasioned its proposal.

Until form is itself capable of requiring the determination of particulars, its claims to authority are arbitrary. But form, presiding over all particulars, universal, neutral, and uninvolved with content, could not act as the determiner of content. The form that was empty without content and the content that was blind without form find their union, not in appearance, but in the symbol. The symbol is heuristic because it embodies content and legislates on the determinate form of the same region of content to which it belongs. (*12*) *The symbol is a legislative actuality.* But its legislation is not from above, or outside, but upon the same region in which *alone* it actually exists. The legislative proposes the same region over which it rules, whether in politics or physics. External legislation is arbitrary, while events not already defined in their mode through order can get no particularization. The business world proposes the laws that regulate it only because every transaction is vaguely in the area of form and seeks its clearer determination within that area.

Wherever there is form, there is a determination of the particular. A work of art is the organization that calls attention to component parts. It reveals particulars. (*13*) *The heuristic force of symbols pervades all forms of language.*

(*14*) *The "real" is that particular which is determined by a symbolic actuality*. The illusory or erroneous is that particular which no symbolic operation can identify. Thus, the distinction, long a source of difficulty, between appearance and reality becomes a function of heuristic form, that is, of actual symbols. What determines an appearance is the same functioning that determines a reality. Thus, the reason for the inconclusiveness of the *Theaetetus* resides in the neglect of the symbolic actuality, in the absoluteness of the difference between the birds of truth and the birds of error.

In idealism such as with Bradley and Royce, the disparity of appearance and reality led to absolute reality.

Skepticism is the failure to find limited reality because no appearance was also a legislative actuality. Skepticism, like idealism, had no yardsticks.

In the case of Kant, his *a priori* space and his other formal modes were proposed as pure form without qualitative particulars and without specific determination. Kant had space, but no yardstick; time, but no clock; logic, but no language. To take his regular walk he would need a clock, not the category of time in the abstract. To tell time one needs a clock. A clock is not a tool or device, but a metaphysical symbol. Every shepherd counts and so has the means of keeping a tally. For that he needs a symbolic artifact, where form and content meet in legislative actuality.

The real is the indeterminant with respect to the procedures of determination, that is, with respect to the appearance of cognitive data. (*15*) *So long as data were "mere" data, not cognitive data, the relation of appearance and reality was arbitrary because their distinction was arbitrary*.

The disinterested datum is "pure," not because it avoids the region of the determinate, but because it establishes it. (*16*) *All disinterested knowledge is pure act*. Purpose-knowledge leads to disappointments. Pure knowledge never disappoints the enterprise in which it is sought. This is the disinterestedness of science or of art. These enterprises are promoted by the particulars, whatever they may be, that ensue upon the heuristic observation and activity. One no longer "saves the appearances," one saves the heuristic discourse. Psychologically controlled purposes, accidental purposes, can be abandoned. But inquiry in accordance with symbolic modes of determining particulars cannot be abandoned. Their imperative is categorical because they determine the difference between appearance and reality.

Consequently knowledge is not the search for reality, but the maintenance of the distinction between appearance and reality. Knowledge is found in the cognitive datum, but if so, in the datum that occurs in the process of determining particulars in one of their symbolic modes.

Knowledge in all its modes, both of nature and of man, finds a common denominator in the processes of particularization, in the continuum of some discourse, in the determination of the specific through the consequences of symbols.

v. The Locus of Necessity

(1) No necessary *answer* can result from an accidental problem. The factors of such a problem are variable. The result is "hypothetical," that is, based on hypothesis.

(2) No necessary *problem* can be proposed by non-necessary factors. Such a problem is accidental.

(3) Empiricism has no necessary answers.

(4) Empiricism has no necessary problems.

(5) Rationalism, based on postulates, axioms, or self-evident "truths," does not, and cannot, define the occasion for proposing such postulates. The occasion for a postulate is not a self-evident truth. No "independent" postulate can *require* another independent postulate. Any statement that is "required" is a sequel, not an original. No postulate is necessary.

(6) Every postulate is *complex* ("Every event has a cause"; "Do unto others"; "If $a = b$, and $b = c$, then $a = c$.") The complexity of any postulate always invokes *nonrationalistic* factors (in the above illustration: events, persons, objects, or situations apropos of which some equality may be discovered).

(6a) No complex can be rationalistic except by abstraction, that is, by assuming the nonrational.

(7) All rationalistic systems have come to seem arbitrary, that is, without ground. (Spinoza, Plato's ideas.)

(8) The idea of an "application" of a rationalistic system is an acknowledgement of its *genetic arbitrariness*. No one asks whether "All mammals are viviparous" has an "application."

(9) Necessity, for this reason, becomes formal and thus arbitrary. It can confess no *genesis* of an intellectual sort. It can have no *intellectual* warrant. Even its application is not intellectually necessary, but accidental. Nor is it clear what one could mean by the applicability of purely formal statements. *Form has no application to a situation that is formless.* No test of "fitness" of a form to the formless could be devised or imagined.

(9a) There is no articulate universal where all content, all individuality, all finitude is problematic. Such a universal is the "undifferentiated homogeneity" of Spencer.

(10) The forgotten condition of all rational necessity and of all empirical contingency is the *individual*. This, of course, is the neglected factor in *all* the philosophy of science and of rational order (logic and mathematics).

(11) The original occasion of all biography is the discovery of the distinction between thought and its object, the me and the not-me, the self and its other (Fichte, Schelling, Hegel; or in terms of history, Vico and his artifacts).

(11a) This distinction must be maintained. This is the basic imperative. It is the ontological and existential component of necessity.

(11b) All formal necessity is the corollary of this original *formal* difference.

(12) All empirical statements are required for the maintenance of this difference. *The necessity of the empirical is the forgotten thesis of rationalism.*

(13) The distinction between self and its other is expressed *only* in artifacts. It is *neither* abstractly rational *nor* accidentally empirical. It is necessarily *not* either of these.

(14) Through formal orders of specific modes this dif-

ference is articulated; for example, logic, mathematics, ethics, and so on. All critical discourse maintains the original distinction. Criticism is only the apparatus for this maintenance. Thus, logic is the self-maintenance of thought through the order of its empirical component. Contradiction is the existential confusion of the original difference. Contradiction is loss of control over the original distinction.

(14a) A *purely* formal "contradiction" is not an existential contradition because the order of consistency is *assumed*. That is why purely formal consistency seems like a game where the rules are assumed. Games fall *within* the radical distinction of self and not-self and do not *define* it. For this reason, too, purely formal orders seek "application."

(14a,i) Note, too, that the "application" is always itself *universal*. It is not like trying on a coat. This shows that the rational systems *do not define the universality* to which they are to apply. They certainly define no *specific* application. They will not be able to define a universal application apart from their own original universality as marking the difference between self and not-self. That is the sole original universality, and the sole original basis for the constitutional necessity of the empirical. *Until the application is necessary it cannot be proposed.*

vi. The Environment of Knowledge

(1) Whatever one talks "about" falls into some environment. If one talks "about" Greylock, one places it in geography, and in all that implies.

(2) If one talks "about" knowledge, one gives it, analogously, an environment. This environment is notoriously hard to pin down, and the usual charge is made that it begs the question.

(3) If one talks about Greylock and says it is 5300 feet high, one can be "corrected." This "correction" operates on an appeal to the assumed environment of Greylock, for example, the established sea level and all the apparatus of location and measurement. All *specific* instances of knowl-

edge are established by the appeal to the assumed environment. Here one finds the play of "contingency" and of the empiricism suitable to it.

(4) But one must avoid the fallacy of composition, treating *all* knowledge on the analogy of its instances (every event has a cause, "therefore," the totality of events has a cause).

(5) One could conclude that one would, then, do well not to talk "about" knowledge at all. This is the conclusion of the mystic (mute).

(6) Even the talk about knowledge needs some status. Some say, "If the truth were told, talk is behavioristic and physiological and so, in the end, physical." Here is an essay in telling the truth that needs no telling and has in the end nothing to do with the telling.

(7) Those who say to one "The truth is not in the telling" put themselves beyond criticism. The truth they propose did not come to *them* through the telling. They own no such dependence. (Repudiation of history.) No fault one finds with the telling disturbs the truth, which, they say, is apprehended apart from all telling. Why must these words win anyone's approval, and how could they, if it were alleged that their teller had no need of them to see whether *he* knew the truth? Shall one say, "I tell it badly but even so, that in no way disturbs my assurance"? Or, shall one say, "I do not understand what you say and even find it 'confused,' but for all that I would not question that you have seen the truth"?

(8) There is much that can be said about the position "I know the truth apart from all telling but, being at leisure, or being paid for my time, etc., I will now use words to tell you about the truth, which, of course, has nothing to do with what was ever said or with my present telling."

(9) Then one encounters, too, the position that it is statements, or "propositions" that are true. Here, the truth becomes a property of what is said and no longer leaves the saying irrelevant to the truth. So, it is no longer true of Greylock that it is 3,500 feet high, but it is a property of a *statement* about Greylock that it is true.

This is the other side of the coin. We now have statements using the word "Greylock" ("the present king of France" was Russell's example) but as to whether or not there is such a mountain, and what one would mean if one were to claim it to be true that there is such a mountain, is left radically obscure. If the truth is *only* in the statement, and not at all in the mountain, then one need make no reference to the mountain in ascertaining the truth of the statement. For the "truth" is now wholly in the statement.

(10) So, the argument advances to a *third* position. It is now alleged that, of course, the statement, if true, or if false, has taken the mountain into some sort of account. The statement "refers" to the mountain and isn't true or false in itself, but only in relation to the mountain.

This mountain, however, being what is referred to by words, is now not to be identified by words. The mountain is no statement but stands apart from *all* statements, including the statement that it is 3,500 feet high. You now don't need mountains to make statements, or statements to identify mountains. You can have a lock for which there is no key, and a key for which there is no lock. (I have some.) It so *happens* that some keys have locks (and vice versa), and some statements have mountains (and vice versa).

But would one then go on to say that *no* key needs any lock (and vice versa)? *This* key has no lock, to be sure, and this lock no key. Would one then conclude that no key needs a lock? Never did? Never will? (Again, perhaps, the fallacy of composition, although I think it another sort of fallacy, not logical.)

(11) So, one finds oneself wanting to keep truth a property of statements, and one wants the statement in some relation to a situation, Greylock, which is apprehended apart from all statements, apart from all symbols.

(12) Apprehension without symbols is, at most, quality. But it is not a place on a map, or an altitude, or a *difference* of quality, or a time. For any such apprehension, one needs symbols, a map, a scale of distance, a measuring operator, an objectification of difference that is functional, a clock,

and all the other apparatus of using these artifactual aids in the apprehension of Greylock.

Were Greylock an *absolute* apprehension, one would need no language or symbol for its apprehension. But it is not absolute.

To "refer" to Greylock would, on these premises, involve the apparatus of identification, and that is linguistic. No identification is absolute. None is qualitative alone. None is unrelational. And all *relation* is symbolic. Any "reference" to Greylock by—or of—a proposition alleged to be true or false is a reference of one symbolic or linguistic artifact to an artifactually defined situation.

A quiet man doing no talking could measure and locate Greylock. But this identification entails symbols (maps, measures). That he has done so, and now can identify Greylock, requires, however, that he employ further symbols. He makes marks on an old map, writes a date on it, or writes, or speaks an account of his researches. He talks about Greylock in terms that are themselves linguistic and artifactual. He can make no statement about an "object" called Greylock until the mountain is artifactually apprehended. No *statement* "refers" to a nonlinguistic situation.

(13) To want the facts without artifacts is to want the absolute. It is to want the nondiscursive.

(14) All objective relations are artifactual, that is, linguistic. That Greylock is 3,500 feet high is a statement that can be checked only apropos of a situation that also makes a statement, in this case, say, a yardstick and numbers. A yardstick is an object that makes statements both possible and necessary. But it is no yardstick as a voiceless datum.

(15) The positions:

a. Truth is in objects, statements and beliefs being incidental and unessential.

b. Truth is in statements alone and not in objects.

c. Truth is in a "relation" of statement to object.

d. Truth is in a discourse that includes both statements and artifactually identified situations.

(16) Conclusion: knowledge has no noncognitively

apprehended environment. The environment of a given statement is always artifactual. There is no nonartifactual cognitive environment. No statement refers to a situation identifiable apart from all statements.

vii. Analysis

(1) Analysis, not being original, requires rules of procedure as a prior assumption. The parts of a chair not only presume the chair but the way of taking it apart. Thus, one reduces it to structural members. If one asks for chemical analysis, one works with the apparatus of reagents, chemical concepts of substance, atoms, valence, weight, volume, etc. Thus, no analysis operates in a vacuum of experience. All analysis entails the *a priori,* i.e., the *functioning a priori* that permits and requires the analysis.

(2) Analysis occurs apropos of the quest for control, and as the extension of control. It has a nonintellectual ingredient. The how-to books tell one how to build a chair by indicating its parts, the relevant dimensions, tools, etc.

(3) All action is analytic because all action is specific and local. One can't act in general. An athletic coach analyzes the components of the activity of swimming, etc.

(4) Metaphysical analysis likewise occurs apropos of control. *Factors in ethics:* pleasure, happiness, others, instinct, calculation, ends and means, egotism, criticism, freedom, mores, loyalty, suffering, the state, law, crime, punishment. *Factors in epistemology:* subjectivity, solipsism, sense, data, illusion, hallucination, error, truth, primary and secondary qualities, cause, probability, logical ideas such as hypothesis, inference, relation, proposition, consistency, fallacy, universals, particulars, individuals, etc. Here, too, the problems occur apropos of the control of statements. Statements get out of control when one does not know the rules of truth telling. One looks for the elements that permit one to avoid confusion, the failure of control, helplessness. One asks whether all statements are logical, e.g., whether statements in history have the same form as those in physics (the repetitive and ahistoric *vs.* the unique and

time-defining, where the date is not a moment in a uniformity but a factor in the revision of what one has taken to be uniform).

(5) Analysis is not, then, the mark of passivity. The analytic consequences, though they may involve data, discover data as factors in the controlled inquiry, or data as in principle such a factor.

(6) Data are discovered apropos of inquiry or of an activity seeking control. We have to *learn* the sensory elements of vision, the difference between visual and aural data, etc.

(7) Quality occurs as one of the orders of objects. Objects are not subsequent to quality but are assumed in their progressive disclosure. Their clarity is mutual. The observation of quality is directed. It is part of a situation that *exists* in terms of such discrimination.

viii. A General Guide to a Modern and Historical Philosophy

(1) The universe is incomplete.

(2) The individual is incomplete, and the incomplete universe is the same as the partial composition of the individual.

(3) A complete universe has been a threat to the individual, however such completeness may have been vaguely imagined.

(4) Vaguely imagined—because any completeness is ineffable i.e., eludes any and all utterance and cannot be spokcn.

(5) The incompleteness is structural, not quantitative, not merely more of the same, as more objects, more places, times, or causes.

(6) The manifestation of the incomplete and of the individual is utterance in any of its modes.

(7) Utterance is the midworld.

(8) The midworld is the actual, neither appearance nor reality.

(9) Utterance is the manifestation and embodiment of local control.

(10) Local control is never complete, either in quantitative extension or in the relation of its modes.

(11) The vehicle of local control is the functioning object.

(12) The primary and ultimate functioning object is the organism.

16

A Few Paragraphs

i. One Culture

Greece invented tragedy as well as geometry, logic, dialectic—all cut from the same piece of cloth: the responsible deed. The common factor of mathematics and drama is the responsible deed, the immediacy allied with and manifesting the universal. There are not "two cultures" but only one. Both art and science fall back on the actual, their common denominator and their source. They are the midworld.

ii. Possibility

There is no "example" of space in a spaceless region where other possibilities are already exemplified but no space is exemplified. Thus space is not a "possibility." Possibility is always limited. To assert a possibility is to do so apropos of a reality. Thus, "the house may catch fire" does not apply to an igloo.

iii. Revelation

There are no criteria for revelations.

iv. The Past

A ship wrecked on a rocky shore has once been afloat.

v. Induction

The usual story about induction (*vs.* deduction) omits the individual who makes the induction. It gives no reason for concerning oneself with coincidental data.

The claim is this: If you want to know nature, proceed inductively. A tricky statement. For nature is not first identified and subsequently explored inductively. All we can know about nature derives from the inductive process. Without a previous idea or concept or sense of nature, there is no basis for the claim that "it" is discovered by an inductive method or process. Nature, then, equals whatever that method discloses. One could not claim that induction furnished the reliable way of finding out the properties of something already present as nature.

vi. Knowledge Never Stops

It would, perhaps, be acceptable to say that mystery begins where knowledge stops. But on its own terms knowledge never stops. Questions may be hard to answer, but so long as a question has authority, an answer is not impossible. Indeed, knowledge is the very citadel of what is not yet known. It embodies its own incompletion. Its controls define and actualize modes of infinity.

vii. Saying So

Nothing is true *because* it is said, but nothing is false without the saying.

viii. Authority

Either one speaks with authority or else one has not spoken at all. There is no "proof" that any person is now, or ever was, present. This is not because the evidence is inconclusive but because none is possible.

ix. Physics

The statement "I am a physicist" is not a statement in physics.

x. Form in Mathematics

One can't count *all* the objects in this room. One would not know where to begin or end, nor could one keep a record of what one had counted if all objects were indifferent, if all were without specific classification, if one could not put a red mark on them with one's *chalk*, used by one's *hand*, with the marked ones laid *aside* or turned marked-side *up*. All that requires a nonquantitative order as a condition of quantity. *Without a nonquantitative order, no quantitative order.*

But neither does one find a nonquantitative variety without implying, and using, quantity. The identification of objects occurs as a quantitative plurality—chairs *and* tables, heavy stones *and* light stones, men *and* women *and* children, young *and* old, chiefs, soldiers, medicine men. Thus the world is full of a *number* of things.

Quantity is no external form applied to nonquantitative objects. There are no nonquantitative objects which can be distinguished. Any situation to which quantity applies is *already quantified*. This is the price of suggesting that quantity *may have* an application. If one shows to what it may be applied, one has already quantified the eligible situation.

Counting occurs as one keeps a tally. Objects are put into a one-to-one correspondence with other objects. For every sheep going through the gate, a pebble. For every carton loaded on the truck, a mark on a tally sheet.

The objects *used* in counting are not treated as objects of a determinate sort. They are only counters, not stones or pebbles, not quartz or flint or carbon or calcium carbonate. It is their use that distinguishes them from passively received data. There is no counting where one has data alone. Counting necessitates the treatment of some objects as nondata, i.e., as functioning objects.

Use means the maintenance of quantitative difference. All alleged quantity is the consequence of counting. Counting is teleological; it is a sign of will. It is the order of one's *actual* world. The world is actual in so far as it is maintained by action.

But this is not purpose. Counting sheep serves a purpose, or counting cartons. One is, perhaps, going to sell ten sheep. But counting in principle serves no purpose. Yet it is an activity. The teleological occurs in activities that serve no purpose. These are *pure* activities. They are *a priori* activities, i.e., they are the form of all special and purposive activity. The selling of sheep needs counting, but it is not the study of the ways of counting; that is mathematics.

Pure activities are not psychological activities, i.e., not accidental. They are environment determining, not environment determined. Nothing in the universe can suggest ten sheep unless one counts, does something, *acts,* takes charge of one's experiences on grounds of one's own. The *a priori* is—in all its forms—self-maintenance of function. The *a priori* is reason, but only a *functioning* reason. It is not purely intellectual. It is no inner intention (Kant). It is the establishment of both inner and outer. One can make a mistake if one counts. One makes no mistake if ten sheep are ten data. The mistake is the revelation of the subjective.

The psychological has not been easily defined. It has no *objectivity*. Nothing objective, we have thought, is psychological. We cannot illustrate it in fact or in the region of facts. We can only show it where there is *act*. But then, only as environment-determining act. The psychological as abstract, as consciousness, fails to give the environment. But as *error* it calls attention to the difference between inner and outer. But it can do this only where the difference is the disclosure of an *activity*. Plato could not find the birds of error; he wanted birds and an aviary, and true birds and false birds, as data, not as the consequence of action, of formal action, of environment-determining action. He wanted a distinction in terms of the intellect alone. Perception and reasoning cannot show in this difference. It is a difference in action, but not in action as response. Kant was right in his idea of the synthetic in so far as this was not passive. One had to do something.

Thus, knowledge, in so far as it involves counting, is a morale factor. It is what one can *do,* what one *must* do; what determines the environment, what also determines the psychological; what joins reason and actuality.

xi. The Abstract

A discourse is "abstract" as a factor of the individual. The "abstract" suggests a prior wholeness, a state of affairs not divided, not separated into its constituents. Quantity, for example, occurs as a separable factor of any action—measuring, telling time, discriminating. Any of the modes of order—physics, psychology, politics—has been "abstracted" from a prior and more inclusive functioning.

The abstract involves the verb "abstracting." Nothing abstract is a datum, an item in the stream of consciousness. Thus the weight of an object is no passive perception. It requires handling, comparing, quantifying. "How much" is never a datum. Passivity does no abstracting.

We abstract from no object unless that object is itself identified in a procedure, in relations, which are never data. Weights or colors as properties of objects entail a procedure of looking, counting, handling.

The individual is no abstraction.

xii. No Data without Structure

Looking for data if data have no structure becomes absurd. Data about the height of Greylock occur in terms of space, and the answer to the question "How high is Greylock?" is given in spatial and numerical terms. Questions are not asked in terms of absolute data; they are asked in terms of the *controls* of data, in this case dependent on a yardstick marked with cabalistic signs like 1, 2, 3.

xiii. Only a Little Space

It is not possible to have only a little space. You have to have all of it in principle if you have any of it. Elea is not the end of the world, nor Chappaqua an absolute beginning.

xiv. Control

Talk all the arithmetic you like and even more than you like, but let the talk keep to that way of talking. To be in control of such statements is to be *in the control of* their inherent order.

xv. Luring

To ask a man what time it is is to lure him into the universal and the actual. He has to "tell" the time.

xvi. Telling the Difference

The philosophy of knowledge is the problem of *how to tell* that one *has* made a mistake, or *not* made one. But one must be able to *tell* the difference. This difference must be in terms of what allows controversy but is not subject to controversy. The difference will not be arguable. The mode of telling that difference will not be arguable. This difference will be the *universal* of epistemology. No philosophy of knowledge can be based on truth. None can be based on error. None can be based on a situation where *this difference* has not been proposed.

xvii. Sentences

Sentences are not "pictures" of reality. Sentences *lead* to action, not to an atomic or complex reality. The unity of fact is in functioning. Nobody can draw a picture of a table *except* under conditions of functioning—*"Look* at it this way." *"Compare* these propositions," and so on. But the table is never a datum, nor is the sentence about it.

xviii. Absolute Negation

How am I to find evidence for an absolute denial? I can deny that Greylock is 5,300 feet high; I do so by appealing to measurement, to space, number, and operations. It is 3,500 feet high. The denial has a basis. An absolute denial has none, any more than an absolute affirmation. One cannot articulate an absolute denial, whereas one can and does articulate the denial that Greylock is 5,300 feet high. It makes sense. An absolute denial has no evidence.

xix. Words

What are the words in a dictionary "about"? Please to speak no word in answering. Does your watch *really* tell time? Use nothing as a revelation of temporal sequence in answering.

xx. Rejection

In a rejection one needs to provide for the occurrence of the belief that one rejects. Otherwise one could allow no force to a rejection. What is rejected must be a miscarriage of a *valid* procedure. Only in terms of an order in numbers could one reject the statement that there is a last prime number.

xxi. The Defense of Freedom

If nature is not our world, evolved from inquiry, it is another dogma. The difference between nature and deity is that nature can be described. It is crucial to save freedom by saving nature as evolved from action, from the actual. The secular state was vague in the middle ages, as were nature study, commerce, banking. But order grew out of action and produced a rival world and a rival discipline. The defense of freedom will have to take the form of defending what freedom has produced.

17

A Catechism for Epistemology

The following "catechism" emphasizes the reversion to the *act* in epistemology, to actual eyes and ears, and so away from abstract data, which leave objects a mystery because out of context with operations that maintain the actual. Empiricism defined through formulae plus sense data seems to me too intellectual, not biological enough. I don't like "objects" to be derivative or order to be *a priori* to the actual. Order is *a priori* only to the intellectual and abstract, and there it must be *a priori*. Both assured form and assured content derive from actuality. Body loses its materialistic menace when it becomes a factor in action, not the object of knowledge or a region indifferent to knowledge.

(1) Why do we associate quality with knowledge?

Because it is through quality that we make mistakes about the content of experience.

(2) Why this emphasis on mistakes?

Because without them our own part in knowing would remain obscure. Without them the need for control over experience would not be suggested.

(3) Are mistakes "made"?

Yes, no mistake is content of consciousness. A mistake is not red or sweet; it is not an apple or an avalanche.

(4) If we make mistakes in the statements and beliefs that involve qualities, why not avoid mistakes by having nothing more to do with qualities? (If lobsters make one ill, why not eat something else?)

Because if we avoid qualities, we can make no true statements either.

(5) But is not quality the means of testing a statement for truth and falsity?

No, not in principle, since both truth and falsity involve quality.

(6) Are not truth and falsity then to be defined apart from all quality?

No, there is neither truth nor falsity without quality.

(7) How then are qualities of any importance to knowing, since they are neutral to both true and false statements?

They are important precisely because they are neutral to both true and false statements and are the vehicles of both. Quality is not to be evaded or treated as an epistemological accident.

(8) Is it not often held that what makes no local difference can be ignored because it is without operational effect, and that it should be ignored because it is "metaphysical"?

It is often so held, but quality cannot be ignored in true and false statements even though it be a universal constituent.

(9) Is it not odd that there should be a universal (quality) that, in principle, makes no local difference, yet is the condition of all local differences?

It is odd only if one rejects local difference.

(10) What is the position of positivists on the idea of local differences?

They stress local difference as of the highest importance in all true and false statements, while at the same time rejecting the metaphysical status of the conditions of local difference.

(11) What follows if local differences have no universal order?

It follows that they are without order, that all differences become absolute, that each alleged difference is itself "metaphysical," and that each difference is inarticulate.

(12) If quality is a universal, is it empirical?

Quality is a universal, but it is not, in principle, empirical.

(13) What is quality as a universal?

It is the universal that permits local difference and is the vehicle of all local differences.

(14) Is a statement true because it is followed by an experience of a quality or group of qualities?

No, the statement "All animals are quadrupedal" is not verified by subsequent qualities like "red" or by all the qualities associated with a red rose.

(15) What sort of sequent quality or group of qualities would verify a statement?

Only those the statement requires.

(16) In so far as a statement entails qualities, do the qualities themselves require other qualities?

No, no quality requires any other sequent quality. The qualities associated with an object (e.g., the color of an animal) do not require any other specific sequent quality.

(17) In so far as a statement is true or false, what is there about it that permits this decision?

A restriction of further experience involving quality.

(18) What is that restriction?

It is the restriction that permits statements involving quality to be made.

(19) Does this mean that there are no statements in terms of quality alone?

Yes, there is no statement in terms of red, sweet, hot, loud.

(20) Does this mean there is no true and false statement in such terms, or no statement?

No statement at all.

(21) How is one to understand any restriction placed upon the qualities sequent to a statement by virtue of which it is to become true or false?

One understands this restriction in terms of nonqualitative elements in the statement.

(22) What are nonqualitative elements in a statement?

They are formal elements.

(23) Are these formal elements wholly alien to qualities?

No, they are the conditions that permit the identification of the various qualities.

(24) Does this mean that qualities are not identified in themselves?

It does.

(25) But aren't qualities entirely original, and even absolute?

No, their very identification is their separation and variety.

(26) Can't variety be defined without qualities?

No, there is no manifold without them.

(27) But is there a unity without them?

No articulate unity; no unity that is not a total blur.

(28) How, then, are qualities identified?

Their original identification occurs through their various modes of control.

(29) What are the controls of qualities? Aren't they just data?

These controls are in their organs—eye, ear, mouth, etc.

(30) Isn't that to take a leap to objects?

Yes, but not to objects in terms of qualities, but in terms of their control and identification.

(31) Does control involve action?

Yes, the qualities are known in their various groupings only by looking, hearing, tasting, etc.

(32) How is this control exercised?

It is an original control, as original as quality itself.

(33) Do these organs restrict qualities?

Yes, a statement in terms of seeing leads to other seeing, not to tasting or hearing.

(34) Does one see one's own eye in order to know that the eye sees?

Not necessarily; one uses one's eye, and in that one controls it.

(35) How then do formal restrictions of qualities enter the picture?

Through use and action alone.

(36) Do use and action imply some nonqualitative element?

Yes, the body as object.

(37) What then is body?

It is the vehicle for the discrimination and classification of qualities.

(38) Does this mean that without body no qualities can be identified?

It does.

(39) Are bodies and their control as original as qualities?

They are. Seeing and things seen are not hearing and things heard, and this distinction occurs through use and control, not through quality alone.

(40) Does such use involve other formal factors?

Yes, the seeing is done with eyes, which are not in the feet; the hearing with ears, which are not in the elbows. Organs are some place. Thus we have the formal factor of space.

(41) What was Berkeley's solution?

He wanted to describe the sense of sight without use of the eyes, and so, of course, his eyes might just as well have been in his feet. This is what comes of talking about qualities without organs, use, control, and bodies. Seeing is a restricted way of identifying qualities and of grasping qualities, only because one can use one's eyes, using one's head instead of one's feet.

(42) Are there other formal elements in the use of an organ?

Yes, one looks *now* right, *now* left, and so encounters the constitutional and formal factor of time.

(43) Are psychological functions related to such use and control?

Yes, it is this element of form that permits memory, attention, interest, learning, emotion, curiosity, etc. This is the reason for the connection between the physiological and qualitative factors in psychology. This relation is necessarily obscure whenever quality is believed discoverable apart from organs, bodies, and other formal elements. It is a relation that must remain obscure so long as quality is supposed discoverable or in any way apprehended apart from use and action and control.

(44) When it is said that there are several senses, or sev-

eral organs, uses, forms, etc., is it to be supposed that these are statements of fact?

No, these are none of them statements of fact. None of these statements falls within an environment. All of these statements concern some element of immediacy. They are all involved in the identification of quality and in the restriction of statements that seek verification in further experience.

(45) If the identification of quality requires the use of organs and so the use of the body, is there any further immediacy of other bodies than one's own?

Yes, one's body as used in observing is part of a continuum of bodies, and this continuum is immediate. It is use that establishes the environment; it is not observation apart from use and action that suggests the environment. Some philosophers have held that observation alone, i.e., quality alone, suggests no distinction between the observer and the observed; in that they may be said to be correct.

(46) On what, then, is our knowledge of the "external world" to be based?

On the activities that involve the senses themselves and their use. It seems plain that an external world without qualities is unknown. It seems plain that quality as supposed passive datum proposes neither the external nor the internal world. The external world is that region of immediacy implied by the identification of qualities and the use of organs.

(47) Is the external world immediate in detail?

No, the identification of quality, and the use of organs occurs only through a variety, which such controlled use explores. The empirical is thus established as necessary, i.e., as part of immediacy.

(48) Are use and control exercised in qualities directly?

No, they are exercised by organs and the body on other bodies, which are in principle immediate, but in their qualitative detail in need of articulation.

(49) In what way, then, is "restriction" as above noted operative in knowledge?

In the maintenance of the conditions of sense experience through the detailing of the immediacy of objects, which are, as above, immediate elements of use and control.

(50) Are objects other than the organs and the body subsequent to quality?

No, the use of organs and their control are always dependent upon other objects, i.e., upon the continuum of the organs and body, this continuum being entailed in the use of organs and in their identification when used.

(51) Is the maintenance of the faculties (seeing, etc.) of some constitutional importance?

Yes, their maintenance is the same as the maintenance of all activity. To lose organs is to lessen the range of activity and of inquiry.

(52) What effect have these statements on the place of the humanities?

The humanities occur apropos of the general position here described. This analysis is philosophical and concerns the general situation in which detailed knowledge occurs.

(53) Can one, then, say that philosophy deals with an "articulated immediacy"?

Yes, it is the articulation of immediacy that alone identifies it. But this entails activity and the use of the senses. The pure reason is the form of self-maintaining functioning.

(54) What is the objective evidence of this functioning?

It is the functioning object that marks a mode of activity. Thus, there are logical and mathematical symbols, those of the natural sciences, institutions, and art, all indicative of some way in which immediacy finds expansion and recognition. Until there are functioning objects the immediate is unknown. Functioning objects of all sorts are the vehicles of form.

18

In Sum

The account one can give of the form of the actual, that is, of local control, is never complete. This is not because there are more things in heaven and earth than are dreamed of in our philosophy. It is not gluttony for more "things," an insatiable appetite, that reveals the inherent finitude and inherent infinity of the act, nor does the question turn on the familiar difficulty of generating statements of the form "All A is B" from "instances." It is rather that we never fully possess ourselves as actual, never fully compose the world, which is the projection of the here-and-now. Modes of organization are not themselves fully integrated. Indeed, organizations may be in conflict, as when the *order* of physics appears not to permit the *order* of history, or the psychological that of logic. This lack of composition appears in dialectical pairs. They stud the philosophical record. There was the problem of the one and the many; we wanted both and each entailed the other, yet their composition was elusive. So, too, with cause and purpose, accident and necessity, substance and attribute, permanence and change, and many more. All those words are organization words, in contrast with denotation words, common nouns, particulars.

In solving a contradiction, one of the alternatives is rejected in order to win clarity and consistency. A dialectical opposition is not solved by exclusion of one of the terms or propositions; it is solved by *uniting* them, by showing their mutuality. Thus, in the case of permanence and change, the apparent contradiction is actually dialectical since the answer must include both. In dialectic the dropping of one term produces confusion. The remaining term is not clarified but vitiated by the denial of the dialectical supplement. This is not so in a logical contradiction.

Hegel, of course, had triads, but I think that the difficulty occurs as a pair. And while such a pair needs a third for its resolution, I prefer to see the third as the state of affairs that enforces the distinction. For an obvious property in a pair is their lack of common ground. Consequently no one says where he stands when he makes the appearance–reality distinction. There is no reconciliation for the simple reason that the distinction has no genesis. And that is important: it is genesis, not a logical or static base, that is required, not another term but a process, not an idea but an actuality.

Then, too, the term "question" suggests an analogy with the sort of problem that does get answered: "How wide is this room?" And it suggests a point of view that deliberates upon the question, as in the case of measuring a particular object. But if the open question be a dialectical pair, then it is not a question that either does or does not have an "answer." The fact is that the dialectical pair is not intelligible. It is a locus of confusion. There is no point of view that can deliberate upon it, think "about" it. The dialectical pair is a threat to the intelligible. If one plays it frankly, one should admit this. If one plays it wisely, one should insist upon it. One should insist upon the claim that no "question" in philosophy has, or could have, an "answer." Philosophy deals in constitutional confusions. To say that confusion is constitutional is to take a step toward the ontological status of finitude. Those who want answers do not want a constitutional confusion. In terms of the question–answer view of knowledge such a confusion could not so much as be described. So, philosophy is a mystery. The historical contribution of radical empiricism and of positivism is that they allow philosophy no refuge short of this constitutional confusion. We are reluctantly driven to the actual.

Every universal has its antagonist, in fact summons it. The self confronts the other self, the subjective the objective, the physical order the moral order, the psychological any order whatsoever, rationalism the empirical, the accidental the necessary, the state the individual, the true the false, the real the illusory, the finite the infinite. From such incoherence and conflict no concluding total order is to be derived. Any universal draws its strength from an opponent, which it must conjure up in order to make good on its own claims to distinctness and authority. Utterance in any universal and composed form simply makes trouble for itself, invites it, cannot evade it.

Is it not well to stay out of trouble? Why court it? It is not easy to regard such conflict as an accident of the self. That seems to be a turning point. The conflict is not to be set aside as irrelevant to one's identity. If one drops it, one is no longer confused, but neither is one so clear. For the concepts in conflict articulate the world even as they muddle it. Purpose and cause mark out regions that enlarge the content of experience. One could not do without them without receding into a primitive fog. In the confusion of conflict one is no non-entity. Rather, one cherishes the difficulty, as if one's self-consciousness required it and was found only there. Conflict does not operate to scatter the self but to establish it, even to organize it. When one encounters "substances"—atoms, the soul—these are invented as names in an essay at organization of particulars. So, conflict seems not the absolute antithesis of organization. It seems that conflict is not unrelated to the essays at organization. And those essays cannot be abandoned. One has, then, a reason to cherish one's conflicts and to find one's identity in them. Conflict finds its integrity in the discovery and maintenance of the very ideas that occasion conflict. We authorize it rather than come upon it.

This seems to me the portrait of the egoist. It is apropos of his own world that the philosopher has conflicts. They are not accidental. They are not forced upon his antecedent placidity, a placidity in which he has recognized himself. They are the man. Nothing antecedently objective can produce his conflicts. Error depends on antecedent assumptions; a conflict embraces the very region alleged to produce it.

So, an egoist, the philosopher is lonely. But this loneliness is no privacy in contrast with any known public domain. This is the true egoism of the philosopher. The very destruction of private and public occurs only among his self-defining conflicts. He is the professional egoist, all others being egoists by accident, whether harmless or fanatical.

The next step, if one could take it, would be an attempt to move the conflict from the ego into the open and public world. The very word "conflict" has a psychic connotation. It is all "in the mind," a bad place for it to be. Well, if not only there, where else? What is the vehicle of conflict?

Now here I am both confident and very obscure. And I use my nostrum. The vehicle of conflict is neither subject nor object, but the midworld, that is, the "artifactual," although I do not quite like that term. Very broadly, there is no conflict apart from the modes of control.

It is said one does not find a "subject." True. But does one find an "object"? The basis of disqualification for both is the same. What we call an object is an experience determined by a type of functioning object, say a yardstick, a clock, a balance, the centimeters–grams–seconds system. Within that system, determined by a type of artifact-controller, one finds nothing individual. The region of nature as order is the implication of functioning objects. These are always themselves continuous with objects, but are treated as determiners, not as things determined. But these controllers exist only in function. The yardstick exists as functioning only. That requires action. It may require purpose, as in measuring for a carpet, or will, as in the study of spatial order in geometry. No region of order is a fact, but rather the resultant of functioning. Nature is a blank apart from the artifactual or symbolic controls that, in functioning, imply that sort of order. Objectivity requires a vehicle, a locus of union of subject and object. For the yardstick is no common noun denoting an object, nor is it an idea "in the mind."

All such controls appear in both nature and mind. But not all function in the same way. One has to act and not react to a stimulus, but in terms of a control defined not by objects in nature, but by objects in function.

There are also artifacts of an individual sort. A work of art is that. What reflective emotion may be is not otherwise to be discovered. Take away art, and one is as impoverished about man as one would be about nature if one destroyed all the yardsticks.

Similarly there are artifacts to which we go for moral order. It was very important to have the law written down, to have ceremony, ritual, holidays, parades, and all sorts of non-natural and non-"mental" vehicles of any actual morality.

There is no conflict between subject and object, mind and body, purpose and cause, once the functioning artifact is accepted as a category. Consider an "error"; what is its vehicle? It has been notoriously difficult to say how an error is possible either in terms of mind or else of body. The old neo-realists were driven to look for objective error, a very reasonable quest if one wants error and nature, too. But I find no difficulty in locating error apropos of the artifactual, in the yardstick in use, or in words. If one cannot find error in the pure object, neither can one in the pure subject. You have to *make* a mistake. It needs a vehicle.

Where you now sit you are surrounded by something made. Those objects are eloquent. Suppose you try to look at "nature" in the raw, without any mediating artifacts; you won't see nature as order. Nature and self are both utter blanks apart from the media that in their function—not in logical implication—lead to them.

The universal is actuality as local control. Any universal entails the verb, as numbers appear in the counting and not otherwise. They are not "perceived." The manifestation of incompleteness and incoherence is in such local control.

That there be a world requires not "evidence" but *manifestation*. This is the articulate immediacy.

The solar system contains no local control. But short of having been counting, short of having walked farther, short of having done so yesterday, no one could have projected or imagined the solar system.

Hear the affronting words: Einstein is quite wrong in calling past, present, and future illusions. He had to *arrive* at that distinction. There is no evidence for it in the stars. The constitutional is enacted, not found or perceived. Short of measuring there is no space. Note the verb. Short of acting there is no past.

Philosophy is not esoteric; it is indigenous. So, if I say I am going to the post office, I am called a philosopher and for the very good reason that in that going I declare a universal order.

In the absence of doing, of the actual, the universal has always collapsed. The radical empiricists do not go to the post office. They are passive—or not even so, since "passivity" is no content of consciousness.

But the act is not a "fact" in the sense of an object come upon. It is a "factum." If no act, then no fact.

But if act is not "perceived," how do we discover it? What is the manifestation of act? What is the *medium* in which we recognize it? This is the "functioning object," the object that is determinative of particular acts. Such is a yardstick or clock, or a word, or any utterance. Here one has a control that is no perceived object. Apart from the functioning object the medium in which the act is manifested has no embodiment.

It was the Greeks who were the founders of science—in the broad sense—because they dealt with the midworld, and so we have Euclid's geometry and Aristotle's logic. They recognized the power of the functioning object. They declared a world on its terms. Say that man is rational; can one say so if there has been no utterance? Rationality is not a fact unless it is a factum. It appears in what has been done. It is, therefore, a *moving immediacy,* not a static quality.

The midworld is the basis for both the individual and what is called the world. On its terms I make mistakes, but also declare why what I made was a mistake.

Shall the incomplete and incoherent claim authority? It cannot be authorized on some other basis than its self-maintenance. A man may approve of me, but on a basis I reject, or disapprove with the same result. We accept criticism only in terms of our own universals. You can catch me out in arithmetic. I am a calculating man myself. This is denied when I am to be found, if at all, apart from my counting. My math is "elementary," in both senses.

We are demoralized today because we proclaim liberty but no actuality as local control and as revelation. Nothing is to be revered. There is no eloquent presence. Our orthodox world is the silent world. The midworld is myth. A myth, an unreality, quarried the stones that stand as the Parthenon or Notre Dame de Chartres. Beat that, if you can, for an incomprehensible marvel. Can myths cut stones?

Well, there are vast consequences. It is the business of a philosopher to discover and organize universals. Any such discovery must then qualify its predecessor universals. This is resisted and I won't say improperly. We cling to whatever world we now have. Einstein balked at dated time, at history. William James, a psychologist, balked at logic. The determinist balks at a constitutional role for the accidental.

I like civility and so I have to fall back on common sense and its validation and not pose as a seer. While the actual, the midworld, the functioning object, the utterance, the accidental as constitutional, the world as incomplete, the world as philosophically defined—while all that may seem very esoteric, it derives from counting my fingers and going to the post office. Intellectuals have no verbs; the common man does. I am joining that common man. And if this is a free country, we'd better get ourselves a metaphysic that has respect for the man on Elm Street. As it is, he is treated with patronage and disdain. Nor does he quite know how to stand in his authority because he is there and therefore projects a world in his doing.

I want the actual to shine and I want to feel the wonder

of a yardstick, a poem, a word, a person. The here-and-now appears to me quite dreamlike unless it can declare the world. I am glad that the dream is dispelled for me.